FROM JENNY TO JET

FROM JENNY TO JET

Pictorial Histories
of the World's Great Airlines

Compiled by

DON C. WIGTON

Designed and Edited by

OCEE RITCH

BONANZA BOOKS · NEW YORK

ACKNOWLEDGMENTS

This book has been made possible only through the fine cooperation of the various airlines and interested persons.

Data and photographs have been made available by the following sources:

American Airlines, Inc., Air France, Braniff Airways, Inc., Canadian Pacific Airlines, Ltd., Continental Airlines, Inc., Eastern Air Lines, Inc., KLM-Royal Dutch Airlines, Lufthansa, Northwest Orient Airlines, Inc., Pan American World Airways, Inc., Qantas Empire Airways, Ltd., Sabena Belgian World Airlines, Swissair Transport Co., Ltd., Trans-Canada Airlines, Ltd., Trans-World Airlines, Inc., United Air Lines, Inc., Boeing Airplane Co., Convair, Douglas Aircraft Corp., Inc., Lockheed Aircraft Corp., Inc., Lycoming Division of AVCO, Northrop Corp., Sud-Aviation, Sikorsky Aircraft Division, United Aircraft Corp.

William Fleming, Stephen J. Hudek, William T. Larkins, Robert Mosher, Stewart Johnson.

CONTENTS

ANNOUNCEMENT

In publishing this book on American airline development, which we call "From Jenny to Jet," I feel that we have complied and made available to airplane enthusiasts and customers of our fine airlines of today a book that will be treasured in the years to come as a valuable pictorial history of the early development of commercial airlines.

When first approached by a well known airplane authority, Don Wigton, I was intrigued by the interesting photographs and the data he had compiled. As a youngster, I was fascinated by the early airplanes and the famous pilots such as the Wright Brothers, Glen Curtiss, the famous Wright aviators such as Ralph Johnstone, Lincoln Beachey, Walter Brookins, Charles F. Willard, Bob Fowler, Ralph Parmalee and others.

In 1910, in Denver, I first saw an airplane fly, and the pilot was the then famous Frenchman Louis Paulhan, who gave an exhibition at Overland Park in Denver in his Farnam Bi-plane with a Gnome rotary engine. I also saw Ralph Johnstone fall to his death in a street alongside Overland Park.

I was so enthused over the possibilities of flying that I went home and built a contraption that I called a Cycle-plane. Pedals operated a small propellor shaft mounted on a luggage carrier above the rear wheel. The rudder was operated by turning the handlebars and the elevator control was by moving the handlebars mounted in a central stem ball and socket joint in an up and down movement. Needless to say, this contraption didn't fly — but it never dimmed my enthusiasm for aviation.

The following year at Walla Walla, Washington, when I was 15 years old, I drove a "cut-down" E-M-F "30" three days during the County Fair in races against Walter Brookins and Charles F. Willard. Brookins flew a Wright Bi-plane, and Willard had a Curtiss with a Gnome engine. On the last day of the Fair, Brookins took me for a ten minute ride over the city. Thus at 15 years of age I became the first passenger ever carried in an airplane in the State of Washington.

I later flew in many of the early commercial airliners and even made one trip to New York during the days when the commercial planes flew only in the day time. I recall getting on at Cheyenne, Wyoming flying to Omaha, Nebr., taking an overnight train to Chicago, and then flying on the next day from Chicago to Pittsburgh.

Later on, after Lindbergh's flight in 1927, I bought a Swallow with a Hisso "E" engine, designed by Lloyd Stearman of Wichita, Kansas. Mrs. Olive Beech, now President of Beech Aircraft in Wichita, was then secretary to Walter Beech, head of Travel-Air. She and a salesman, a Mr. Christopher, tried to sell me a Travel-Air, designed and built by Walter Beech, whom she later married. Mr. Beech was the designer and builder of the Travel-Air and the company name was later changed to Beech Aircraft.

To those of us who have watched the development of the airplane from the days of the Wright Brothers to the highly perfected planes of today it seems unbelievable that such tremendous strides could have taken place in so short a time. I hope you enjoy this book as much as we did in compiling it.

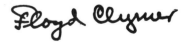

QANTAS, pioneer Australian airline began operations with lone AVRO 540-K, in 1920.

4

AIR FRANCE

AIR FRANCE was formed in August 1933 by the merging of five large existing French air-transport firms.

The Company's history thus goes back to the origins of commercial aviation in France, that is to say to the period immediately after the first world war.

I. Origins

At that time the machines merely served the European countries bordering on France, and North Africa; for this latter journey only mailbags were allowed on board, since flying over the sea represented too great a risk for the embarkation of passengers.

As early as December 1918, "Latecoere Air Lines" made a first survey flight from Toulouse to Barcelona with a Breguet 14, a preface to the establishment of a line to Africa and South America. A few months later, on the 8th of February, 1919, Lucien Bossoutrot, a "Farman Lines" pilot, achieved the first air transport of passengers between Paris and London. It was the first international air transport in the world. The machine used was a "Goliath", a military aircraft converted into a commercial one by the equipping of a closed cabin which could take thirteen passengers. The same month, "Farman Lines" also connected Paris and Brussels.

These results then acted as an incentive on pioneers, and air transport firms multiplied. In 1920 three companies were competing on the Paris-London route. For greater efficiency they united and three years later formed "Air Union."

In Eastern Europe and in the Balkan States the "Compagnie Franco-Roumaine de Navigation Aerienne" undertook survey flights between Paris, Prague and Warsaw, and opened a Paris-Prague service. "Farman Lines" chose to turn their attention to Northern Europe, and their Paris-Brussels service led them to push on towards Holland. Meanwhile "Latecoere Air Lines" pursued their exploration southwards.

Finally, other small companies opened different lines of varying interest: for example Paris-Geneva, Nimes-Nice, Bayonne-Bilbao, and Paris-Cabourg.

The government, realizing the value of this new means of transport, looked approvingly upon the achievements of all these private firms. It helped them by the concession of lines and by grants in the form of subsidies for the purchase of materials or for the operation of certain routes.

These joint efforts issued in encouraging results. Whereas in 1920 only 942 people travelled by plane, the number of passengers reached almost 20,000 in 1925. Five years later, in 1930, the structure and economy of French air transport were markedly different.

By that date, in fact, doing pioneer work and opening new lines had made remarkable progress, especially in Europe. The needs of regular operation had persuaded the companies to strengthen their means. It resulted in a search for an agreement with certain foreign companies: an early example was the pool agreement[1] between "Farman Lines" and the German company D.L.H. on the Paris-Cologne-Berlin route in 1926.

Another result, on the national level, was the concentration of firms. The five which remained served a network covering almost the whole of Europe and some African and South American areas.

On these latter routes, however, only mailbags were carried. The postal traffic which today seems of secondary importance in the total figures was a determining factor in the beginnings of air transport. In particular all the efforts which, in 1930, resulted in the crossing of the South Atlantic by the Mermoz-Dabry-Gimie crew in a Late 28 in 19 hours 35 minutes are indebted to it. The "Compagnie Aeropostale" which had taken over from "Latecoere Air Lines" succeeded in establishing the link between Toulouse and Santiago in Chile.

CIDNA "Compagnie Internationale de Navigation Aerienne" took over, in 1925, from the "Compagnie Franco-Roumaine de Navigation" which as early as 1923 had inaugurated night passenger services between Belgrade and Bucharest; it provided a regular service between Paris and the great capitals of Central and Eastern Europe, Prague, Warsaw, Bucharest, Istanbul, Belgrade, Sofia and Vienna were thus successively served. A survey flight over Moscow was a complete success, though not followed by a regular service. Leaving Europe, the Company's network extended as far as Ankara, Baghdad, and even, in the course of a survey flight, Teheran.

SGTA, "Societa Generale des Transports Aeriens" successor to "Farman Lines" improved the service to Northern Europe. A direct Paris-Berlin service was in operation as early as 1928: two years later the first night link was inaugurated between the two cities. Meanwhile the Paris-Cologne-Hamburg-Copenhagen-Malmo route was opened, which thanks to the Farman 300 "Silver SK", put Sweden eight hours away from France.

"Air Union" concentrated its efforts on Domestic and Mediterranean routes. Profiting by the efforts of "Aeronavale" which had opened on Antibes-Tunis-Bone service, the company organized Marseilles-Ajaccio-Tunis links and successfully conducted a survey flight from Marseilles to Central Africa over Egypt, the Sudan, the Sahara and Tunisia. In France the company organized Paris-Lyons-Marseilles and Marseilles-Cannes services; further, it inaugurated international Lyons-Geneva and Paris-Geneva links, and continued its regular Paris-London flights.

Its subsidiary company "Air Orient" undertook the laborious pioneering of the Far Eastern route, where Maurice Nogues distinguished himself. The first Marseilles-Damascus-Saigon service was opened in January 1931. The journey from France to Indo-China took ten days, first with a Liore-Oliver 242 over the Mediterran-

---

[1]A pool agreement provides for the pooling and sharing of earnings according to a ratio previously arranged. It, therefore, does not suppress competition, but reduces it.

DE HAVILLAND *DH4*, ex WWI fighter, was used by several companies. Top speed: 90 mph.

ean and then for the rest of the way with a Breguet w80. There were two departures a month.

From then on, French commercial aviation figures put it in the front rank of all Europe. It established routes over four continents: Europe, Africa, South America and Asia. Its activity in 1932 can be summarized thus:

Miles flown	5,780,000
Passenger-miles flown	13,944,000
Short ton-miles of freight carried	420,000
Short ton-miles of mail carried	310,000

The authorities, foreseeing not only the development of traffic but the extension and creation of routes to China, Madagascar and North America, then contemplated to give French civil aviation the benefit of a charter in order to make effective aid possible. Thus was drawn up the law of December 11, 1932.

Nevertheless, although scarcely out of the pioneer era, international air transport soon saw its life dominated by the fierce competition to which the companies of different countries were given up. To allow our civil aviation to cut a better figure in this struggle, the authorities urged the regrouping of the existing large firms.

II. The Founding of Air France

So, in 1933, the merging of "Farman Lines", "CIDNA", "Air Union", "Air Orient" and the re-purchase of "L'Aeropostale" resulted in the founding of "Air France."

The new corporation made up a network of 23,600 miles. "Air France" exerted itself to coordinate the routes operated by its predecessors, simplify its interchange systems, increase the frequency of its services, open new ones, perfect its fleet and make it more homogeneous.

The last problem meant a complete renewal of all the materials in use. The fleet bequeathed by the old companies numbered 259 machines, unfortunately odd and for the most part obsolete. In particular single-engined planes greatly outnumbered those with more than one engine. By substituting these for single-engined types "Air France" sought to standardize the machines used on its routes and to reduce their number, because of their increased weight carrying capacity and speed of operation.

In 1939 there were 90 machines in the fleet, 15 of them sea-planes. They were all made in French factories and could compete with the best foreign products in technical perfection as well as in comfort and safety. In six years the speed increased from 124 to 186 miles an hour. Aircraft like the Dewoitine D. 338, which was used in particular on the Far East route, offered 24 passengers spacious seats.

To keep this working stock in good repair the management of the Company paid special attention to the setting up of a technical organization adapted to its new needs and resting upon three principal centers at Le-Bourget, Toulouse and Marignane. The workshop specializing in engine-overhaul was established at Rognac (Bouches-du-Rhone), while the machines allotted to the transatlantic route were maintained at Dakar and Buenos-Aires.

Air safety made great progress too. For one thing, methods of piloting aircraft steadily improved. On the other hand, constant evolution made possible the use of new equipment for piloting air navigating and blind landing. These results were owed essentially to technical progress and to the sacrifices made by the crew, sometimes of their own lives. Such was, in particular, the fate of Nogues, Bajac, Genin, Mermoz and Guillaumet. They bear witness to the contribution made by French civil aviation to the development of international air transport.

"Air France" thus achieved intercontinental transport in completely new conditions for world economic relations. In 1934 it opened the first all-air commercial service between France and South America. It was in fact the crossing of the South Atlantic by "L'Arc-en-Ciel" (May 28, 1934) which made this link possible. Towards Africa, a regular passenger service was inaugurated in 1936 between Paris and Dakar. In this region the "Regie Air Afrique", formed in 1934, operated routes which extended those of "Air France" as far as Madagascar. In 1938 the Far East route was pushed as far as China and reached Hong Kong. The journey between Marseilles and Hong Kong lasted eight days. In Europe and the Mediterranean new services multiplied. Paris-Stockholm became a regular service in 1936. In 1939 a plane left Paris for London every hour. Mail transport also witnessed some successful innovations. Night mail services Paris-Toulouse and Paris-Marseilles were successively inaugurated in 1937 "Air France" took part in the reorganization of "Air Bleu", which specialized in mail transport in metropolitan France. In the same year "Air France" and the "French Line" created a company especially entrusted with the study of future routes on the North Atlantic. "Air France Transatlantic" successfully conducted several survey flights linking Europe to North America by way of the Azores and Bermuda. The last of these flights took place on August 27 and 28, 1939.

Then, the war broke out overthrowing the activity and structure of "Air France."

III. The Ordeal of War

From the month of September, 1939, the aircraft staff and plant of the Company were put at the Government's disposal to play their part in the war effort. After the 1940 armistice a few regular links were established between the free zone of France, North Africa and Africa.

The network in Metropolitan France comprised a Vichy-Lyons-Marseilles-Toulouse-Vichy circuit. Among African routes was established the Marseilles-Dakar link, either by way of Mauritania or by Algiers and Niamey. There were still local networks in French West Africa and Indo-China.

Nevertheless, this period saw the birth of the law of September 19, 1941, an important stage in the control of air transport. This law lays down in particular the principles of state supervision over air navigation firms.

In 1942 the enemy occupation of the whole country led those who could to regather in North Africa. Such means of air transport as existed were requisitioned by the authorities. This brought about the formation of T.A.M. ("Transports Aeriens Militaires") organized in three networks. The central network was based on

KLM Dutch airline flew hardy passengers in De Havilland *DH-9.*

Algiers, the eastern on Damascus and the western on Dakar. The important thing for the Allies at that time was to win the war, and these services proved themselves valuable auxiliaries to the army.

Immediately after the landing of troops in France in 1944 a fourth network was set up in Metropolitan France, and all four came under the name of "Reseau des Lignes Aeriennes Francaises" (R.L.A.F.). This organization remained closely attached to the Air Ministry, and answered needs similar to those met in the United States by "Air Transport Command."

The end of hostilities brought a return to a more normal situation. From the beginning of 1946 direct state administration gave way to autonomous activity by "Air France", which again found itself entrusted with the operation of all French air routes. Still, the company emerged much changed from these testing years. In particular the authorities had in June 1945 decided to nationalize it and entrust to Parliament the business of drawing up its new charter.

IV. The "Compagnie Nationale"

This charter is in fact to be found in the law of June 16, 1948 which sets up the "Compagnie Nationale Air France." The legislator was at pains to distinguish the nationalized undertaking from a state-controlled firm.

A sign of this intention may be seen in the constitution given to the firm and even in the division of capital. The Company's property belongs to the nation, so its capital stock is divided among public bodies (state, departments, communes . . .) and private individuals. The state naturally holds the preponderant part. The general trend throughout the world has in fact been for governments to control air transport more and more closely, either by operating the routes directly or by issuing very strict rules for their operation. This has allowed the creation, as has happened in France, of private air transport companies side by side with the national company.

For the last ten years the dominant factor in the company's life has been its spectacular expansion.

In the year 1948, the firm employed 11,150 people; in 1958 it employes 20,000. This development in staff illustrates the multiplication of new tasks and also underlines the importance that has accrued to problems of personnel policy, its selection and training.

The company formed for air transport has also become a great industrial concern. Maintenance and overhaul workshops occupy a considerable place. Over 6,000 engineers, technicians and craftsmen work to keep the fleet airworthy. "Air France" technical plants are reckoned among the best equipped in the world. Specifically, they cover 109,600 square yards at Orly alone for the maintenance and overhaul of the fleet and its equipment. In the suburbs of Paris there is the Courbevoie plant, where engine-specialists of international reputation and authority repair engines not only for the Company but also for foreign clients who are anxious to find high-quality workmanship. At Toulouse there is a center concerned with the maintenance and overhaul of two-engined DC 3's and four-engined DC 4's. At Le Bourget are maintained the machines allotted to mail transport. Finally at Dakar, Brazzaville, Tananarive, Fort-de-France and Algiers there are work-

shops more modest in extent, but equipped with modern tools, to look after the fleets which work the local networks outside France.

The development of this industrial branch is naturally linked to the growth of the fleet needed to face new activities.

Immediately after the war the plane in service were Bloch 220's, Dewoitine D 338's, Lockheed 60's and Ju 52's. "Air France" progressively replaced them with French built planes, like the Languedoc 161's, or with planes of American origin like the Douglas DC 3's, the Douglas DC 4's and the Lockheed 749 A's "Constellation." There was thus achieved, in particular with the last make named, a marked increase in comfort and performance: the "Constellation" was the first pressurized airliner. Modernization continued with the putting into service in 1953 of four new types of machine: one American, the Lockheed L. 1049 "Super Constellation"; one French, the Breguet "Provence" Deux Pants Br. 763; and two British, the Vickers "Viscount", the first turbo-jet machine, and the Comet I, the first jet airliner. (This latter was withdrawn from service after a few months.)

In 1957 arrived the Lockheed L. 1649's "Super Starliner." These four-engined American machines were the last word in conventional aircraft. Their wing-design allowed these long-haul machines to cross the North Atlantic non-stop with 70 passengers on board.

In succeeding years, the French Company has operated twin-jet Caravelle SE 210's and four-jet Boeing 707's "Intercontinental". In speed and capacity these machines are much superior to conventional aircraft: characteristics which underline the deep transformation of air transport in our time. It is becoming an excellent means to the spread of goodwill in international relations, since a large part of world air traffic is concerned with regular air services between foreign countries. In this respect the network seems a determining factor in a company's position. "Air France" has been able, not without great effort, to actuate the greatest total length of unduplicated air routes in the world. In 1946 it opened Paris-New York and Paris-Buenos Aires transatlantic routes and resumed Paris-Saigon services. In 1952 it extended this Far Eastern route as far as Japan and inaugurated a Paris-Mexico link. In the following year service to Central America began with a route to Bogota (Columbia). Then, in 1954 the Company energies were turned towards Northern Europe with links between Paris and Scandinavia. Finally, 1958 saw the opening of the polar route from Paris to Tokyo, a 30 hours' journey with a single stop at Anchorage. In the same year the Paris-Moscow route was inaugurated and the Paris-Bogota services were extended to Quito and Lima.

This brought the total length of the "Air France" network to 191,300 miles. About 20% of this total represents the length of the local networks outside France. The company has in fact set up in French West Africa, French Equatorial Africa, Madagascar, the Antilles, Algeria and the Sahara local networks whose traffic figures do little justice to the services of the first railways to the French provinces in the nineteenth century. More particularly, in these countries, "Air

Landing fields were just more of sun-baked prairie for QANTAS 'airliners' in 1920's.

France" also plays a part in the planning and carrying out of ground facilities and in the setting up of a tele-communications network. In other words, the aero-plane, especially overseas, acts as an economic incentive.

To facilitate the functioning of a network spread over four continents, "Air France" has set up twelve Regional Flight Services (S.R.V.). They play an important role in their own regions it is their business to prepare flights, to watch over aircraft in the air and to take all necessary measures if a delay or an unforeseeable alteration changes the normal flight programme. These Regional Flight Services form a ground backbone for air operations: they give precious help to the crews in charge of the flights.

"Air France" bent all its energies in the training of flying staff. In fact this duty has fallen to it not only for its own needs but also for the needs of the whole body of French air transport. The installation of flight-simulators allows, with all possible economy and speed, the conversion and qualification of flying personnel in new types of machines as they are put in service.

Another feature of air transport since the end of the war can be seen not so much in the industrial or operational field as in the commercial one: the fierce competition between the largest air transport companies in the world. It is easily explained. Their custom has considerably increased — from 18 million passengers in 1946 to 87 million in 1957. But that is still a very small part of people who could board a plane. Although air transport has been able to command attention for the advantages it offers the user — speed, comfort and safety — it has not yet, in spite of a policy of lower prices, conquered public at large. It is from the struggle for this conquest that competition was born. "Air France", on its part, lays stress on the need for dynamic commercial action. In many foreign countries agencies of the Company represent it to the local clientele. Further, travel agencies provide precious assistance in this work of customer-relations. This organization is completed by the establishment in Paris of a central booking service equipped with the very latest improvements in the way of intercommunication.

Though well provided, "Air France" does not forget the deep-seated solidarity between air transport companies. Here our Company's role in international organizations is worth underlining: specifically, within the I.A.T.A. (International Air Transport Association) our delegations have an effective mediating role which has on several difficult occasions made possible the subordination of legitimate but private interests to the general interests of the profession and the public.

"Air France" believes, because its history teaches it so, that air transport will grow if it can unite the momentum of expansion and the discipline of co-operation.

This is truly not the end of the story about Air France over the world. In a word, you have been reading the opening chapters of a story spanning thirty-eight years of experience in the field of air transport. If the Frenchmen whose acumen wrote the story had been willing to draft a "final page" in their pursuit of one of the great human endeavors — aviation — then the final word would not have spelled success.

For success today, and the many "today's" throughout the history of Air France from 1919 forward, have brought the public accolade expressed in terms of millions of passengers, simply because the executives and leaders of the French Airline have always considered the present as a guide to a flexible definition of what must be planned for tomorrow. A glance backward has prepared for a searching study into tomorrow.

In brief, here begins the story of Air France in the field of air transport, a new departure into the jet era with plans laid on the firm foundations of almost four-decades of leadership. It is the beginning in a French word — aviation — an international word to share with the world and with you.

Early passenger comfort attempts were made with cabined AVRO Triplane used by QANTAS.

Early TWA mailplanes, Douglas M-2's, could also accommodate two passengers.

Personalized aircraft: This Swallow, operated by United, has "Franklin Rose" lettered below cockpit.

14

Pitcairn *Mailwing*, was built by Harold Pitcairn in order to accept airmail contract won in successful bid. Pitcairn Aviation later became Eastern Airlines.

15

Waco J-6 served Northwest Airways on mail route out of Minneapolis.

AMERICAN AIRLINES

IN THE first phase of the commercial air industry's growth, after the First World War, airplanes had little economic significance. The first Army-flown air mail had been established by the U.S. Post Office Department in 1918. The first passenger plane built as such had appeared in 1919. But until the passage of the Kelly Air Mail Act in 1925, passenger air transportation was a disorder of charter flights and Sunday joy-hopping. There were a number of small companies, irregular in their operations, precariously financed. The airways were primitive. They were un-lighted. Night flying was a wild adventure. The plane was severely limited in it's utility. It could not fly safely in bad weather.

The Kelly Air Mail Act authorized the Post Office Department to let contracts to private companies for carrying the mail. And this was the start that this new form of transportation needed.

The first two contracts went to American Airlines predecessor companies — to Colonial Airlines to fly the mail between Boston and New York. And to Robertson Aircraft Corporation to fly it between Chicago and St. Louis.

On April 15, 1926 . . . "That momentous afternoon in April" — as Lindbergh describes it . . . Robertson inaugurated air mail service between St. Louis and Chicago.

Lindbergh used a De Havilland DH-4 biplane on that first flight. That was the first **scheduled** flight for what eventually became American Airlines.

In 1928, the Universal Aviation Corporation was set up and began acquiring the stock of six airlines. One of these pioneer outfits was Robertson, which had started out seven years before with a single Curtiss biplane and by them was operating the mail runs between St. Louis and Chicago, and St. Louis and Omaha. And there were Braniff Air Lines, operating between St. Louis and Dallas and other small airlines.

First capital stock of Robertson in 1921 was $15,000 and was issued originally for the one Curtiss biplane, with one Curtiss OX-5 engine, two complete sets of parts for the engines, miscellaneous spare parts, a lease on ground — presumably an airport site at Robertson, Mo. — and miscellaneous contracts for advertising.

In 1930, the Aviation Corporation — a $35 million firm — bought control of Universal Aviation Corporation and two holding companies. The result was a system of routes notable for it's lack of system. The subsidiary airlines operated independently and often competitively. The routes went from coast to coast but not in a straight line and connecting routes were a rarity.

An effort to bring some order to the route patterns had to be made. On January 25, 1930, the Aviation Corporation consolidated the subsidiary airlines by forming American Airways. Operationally, however, the consolidated airline was still split into four independent divisions — Colonial, Embry-Riddle, Southern Air Transport and Universal — which was headquartered in St. Louis.

In 1932, an operations group was set up for the whole system, and this was American's first centralized Operations Department. Chosen as vice president to head the new operations department was C. R. Smith, who had established an enviable record as head of southern division operations. Two years later Smith was named president of American Airlines, and he is president of the company today.

Going back — in the Universal group, besides Robertson, were Braniff, organized in 1928 (a different company from the Braniff operating today), Continental Air Lines (no connection with the Continental Air Lines of today), organized in 1927, Mid-Plane Sales and Transist Co. Northern Air Lines, Inc., Northrop Airplane Company, Air Transportation, Inc., Central Air Lines Co., Egyptian Airways Co., Robertson Flying Services, Inc., Universal Air Lines, Inc., and Universal Air Lines System Terminal Co.

Quite a bit is actually known about early aviation history in St. Louis, the problem is that it is not written down. Harold Otto joined the company in 1930. Otto was with Universal in Kansas City in the late twenties, and as a matter of fact, for a few months in 1930 was one of four pilots chosen as "couriers" to serve on flights. It was not until 1934 that the first stewardesses were hired.

Nonstop flights 1 and 2 between St. Louis and Chicago were called the "Skyline Limited" and were operated with Fokker Super-Universal six passenger cabin monoplanes. Air mail was carried in a separate compartment — which meant the passengers did not have to sit on air mail sacks, as they still did on some runs. And extra fare of $3.00 was charged on the "Skyline Limited" flights.

The first "new" planes Robertson acquired were Douglas Mailwings, modeled after the Army round-the-world planes. By the end of 1927, Robertson operated five DH's, three Douglases, one Standard and one Waco. The Travel Airs were bought in 1928. The pilots got the mail through — even if it took all night. Walter Braznell, now assistant vice president-flight for American, recalls the most landings he ever made between St. Louis and Chicago was 12.

The earliest pilots of passenger planes were not uniformed. But the first attempt at a uniform for pilots was produced by Bud Gurney (in charge of flying personnel) who came to Lambert Field attired in a blue coat, white flannel trousers and a chauffer's cap with the initials of the airline on it.

In 1936 — American introduced the famous Douglas DC-3, still used in many parts of the world, although retired by American in the late forties in favor of more modern airplanes.

The following is quoted from a 1954 by C. R. Smith before the Newcomen Society.

As the industry came into the "thirties", external struts, wires, and fabric gave way to all-metal construction. Aircraft power plants reached new efficiency with the development of the air-cooled radial engine. There was greater horsepower per pound of engine. And

Stearman Biplane was Trans-Canada Airlines workhorse for many years.

this, in turn, made possible bigger and faster aircraft — speeds of more than 100 miles per hour.

Aviation was moving toward more efficient shapes in aircraft — toward the modern airliner — but this did not come overnight. Instruments, radio, were adequate for their day — but by today's standards, they were rudimentary. The cost of operating was very high, the financial supports of the industry were uncertain, passenger travel was not yet a business. American, and the industry, had to depend, for survival, on mail pay and subsidy.

In February, 1934, came the virtual end of the first phase in airline development. The Post Office Department cancelled the Air Mail contracts. The cancellation lasted two months. When new mail contracts let, the Country had an air transportation system that was just that — systematic, and cohesive. And American Airways, with it's southern transcontinental route, had become American Airlines. The following month, American introduced the industry's first sleeper service. At the same time, the Company's first stewardesses began to fly on the line. And food service was introduced. American believed that selling it's product, air transportation, was fully as important as producing it. And the Company started to implement that belief.

Though the transport plane has grown in size and range and speed, the streamlining of it's air surfaces has remained essentially unchanged from that of the Douglas DC-3. The DC-3 was, for it's day, the perfect transport. It struck the balance that airline engineers search for in speed, in gross weight, in power and payload space and wing area. It permitted economies that had been beyond the Company before.

With the Douglas DC-3, the name "Flagship" was born, and eventually American's Flagship Fleet consisted of 94 of these planes. The first of these planes was put into service in June, 1936. These were important years, critical years for American. Research that had been going on, unceasingly, since the "twenties" was producing improvements that the Company had to have to grow. Full-feathering propellers were put on the Douglas DC-3's. American tested the first Instrument Landing System, and developed and tested the automatic radio direction finder. High-octane aviation fuel had been developed. Real headway was being made in conquering the problem of transmitting flight and reservations information at high speed from one end of the Country to the other.

The second World War brought the industry, and American, into an entirely new phase of development. Within six months after Pearl Harbor, more than half of the airlines industry's fleet of fewer than 400 planes had been sold or leased to the Government.

All through the "thirties", American had confined itself to operating within the geographic limits of the United States of America. But, in 1941, the company inaugurated service to Toronto, Canada; and, a year later, with the Country at war, it pushed an airline south of the border to Monterey and Mexico City.

With the war over, the air transportation industry took stock of itself. What it saw was more than promising. Under the emergencies of war, the air industry had acquired decades of experience in a matter of a few years. Flights of very long distances were commonplace. The operators had learned how to carry heavy cargo. There were navigation aids that five years before would have seemed improbable, or years away — radar and Ground Control Approach. A whole generation, millions of people, had been brought to a realization of what the plane meant, and what it could do.

DeHavilland *DH-50* was four-seater capable of cruising at 80 mph.

De Havilland *DH-61* carried eight in cabin over Austrailian bush country.

Fokker, famed manufacturer of WWI fighter aircraft, quickly turned to peaceful pursuits at end of conflict. This F-2 in service of KLM carried four and pilot.

Dornier *Merkur* ushered in luxury air travel for Lufthansa, German airline.

Merkur, also used by Swissair, cruised at 109 mph with ten aboard.

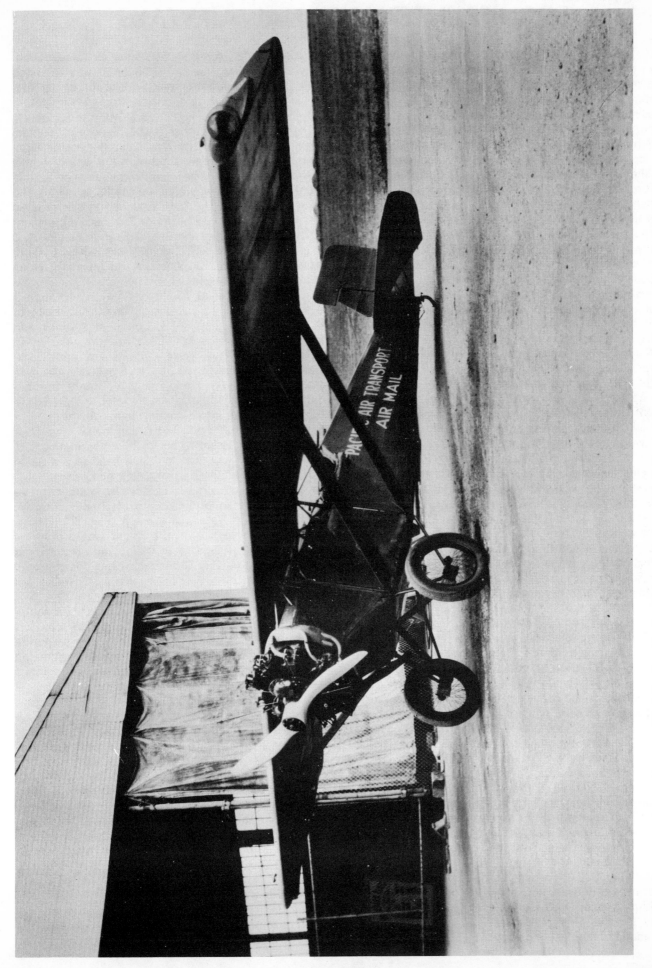

Ryan M-1 used by Pacific Air Transport, pioneer West Coast organization later a part of United Airlines, was forerunner of Lindberg's famous "Spirit of St. Louis".

BRANIFF INTERNATIONAL AIRWAYS

BRANIFF International Airways, the largest air carrier based in the Southwest, operates 18,432 miles of domestic and international air routes through 16 states and the District of Colombia in the United States and 10 Latin American countries.

The airline was founded in Oklahoma, June 20, 1928 by the late Thomas E. Braniff. On that date the first Braniff flight, a five-passenger Stinson-Detroiter, flew the 116 miles between Tulsa and Oklahoma City. The present Braniff Airways was incorporated in November, 1930, and the real impetus to Braniff's growth came in 1934 when the airline received its first mail contract from Chicago to Dallas via Kansas City, Wichita and Oklahoma City in May of that year.

Throughout more than three decades, Braniff has developed into a major U.S. airline serving the entire Midwest as well as major cities in the Mid-South, Washington, D.C. and New York. Braniff's name entered the international realm with the inauguration of its first service to Latin America in 1948.

Braniff's expansion began shortly after its first mail contracts were received. In January, 1935 Braniff bought the Long and Harmon Air Service which held mail contracts to serve ten Texas communities. The company then became known as the "Great Lakes to the Gulf" route, operating more than 3,000 route miles and flying almost 13,000 miles daily.

In 1935 a fleet of 10-passenger, twin-engine Lockheed Electras were put into service and traffic continued to grow on the Texas-Chicago route. In June, 1937, 14-passenger Douglas DC-2 aircraft were put on the line, and in 1940 a fleet of 21-passenger Douglas DC-3 planes went into operation.

During World War II, Braniff gave up more than half its fleet to the government for military use. The company flew contract routes to the Panama Canal Zone and domestic military routes for the Air Transport Command and held training schools for Army pilots, radio operators and mechanics.

Braniff's general offices were moved from Oklahoma City to Love Field, Dallas, Texas, in 1942. After the war, the DC-3's were returned to the company and a fleet of four-engine Douglas DC-4's was bought from the government and converted into 48-passenger liners.

Expansion of service to additional cities throughout the Midwest continued after World War II, and in May, 1946, the Civil Aeronautics Board awarded Braniff 7,700 miles of routes in Latin America for service to the countries of Cuba, Panama, Colombia, Ecuador, Peru, Bolivia, Paraguay, Brazil, Argentina and Mexico. Bi-lateral air treaties were completed between the United States and most of the countries. Before service could begin, Braniff had to build its own system of navigation and communications facilities across the ocean, jungle and mountains. Today, it has more than a half million dollars invested in the most powerful and modern radio network now operating in Latin America. Six 52-passenger DC-6 sleeper liners were bought, primarily for the international service, and three more were added to the fleet late in 1951.

In June, 1948, service was begun as far as Lima, Peru via Cuba, Panama and Ecuador. It was extended to La Paz, Bolivia in February, 1949; to Rio de Janeiro, Brazil in March, 1949; to Asuncion, Paraguay in March, 1950; to Buenos Aires, Argentina in May, 1950; and to Sao Paulo, Brazil in October, 1951. Service to Bogota, Colombia and Mexico City was delayed pending completion of bi-lateral treaties between the United States and those countries. The commercial aviation agreement with Colombia was signed in October, 1956 and service between the U.S. and Bogota was inaugurated by Braniff in May, 1957. The U.S.-Mexico agreement was completed in mid-1960 and Braniff inaugurated new one-carrier service between Minneapolis-St. Paul, Kansas City, Dallas, San Antonio and Mexico City on November 9th of that year.

The first of a fleet of 25 Super-Convair 340 aircraft was delivered to Braniff in July, 1952. On August 16 of that year, the merger of Mid-Continent Airlines and Braniff Airways, which had been approved earlier in the year by the Civil Aeronautics Board and stockholders of both companies, became official. The new company retained the trade name of Braniff International Airways which the airline adopted in 1946 with the granting of the international routes. At the time of the merger, Braniff had 2,857 employees and Mid-Continent 1,239. Braniff served 29 cities in the U.S. and nine in Latin America. Mid-Continent served 32 in the U.S. and six of these also served by Braniff.

On January 10, 1954, T. E. Braniff, founder, president, and Chairman of the board of Braniff Airways, was killed in a private plane crash near Shreveport, Louisiana. Three days later, the Braniff board of directors held a special meeting in Dallas and elected Fred Jones of Oklahoma City Chairman of the Board. Chas. E. Beard was elected President, and J. W. Miller became Executive Vice President.

In 1955 attention was focused on future flight equipment plans, and Braniff's management also took forward-looking steps in matters of expanded corporate financing, improved ground facilities and strengthening of schedule patterns through equipment interchange agreements with other major U.S. air carriers.

Two major developments in Braniff's route pattern occurred in 1955 and 1956. As the result of the CAB decision in the New York-Balboa case, Braniff and Eastern Air Lines in August, 1955, inaugurated new through one-plane air service between New York and Washington, D.C., and key cities in Panama and on both coasts of South America through an equipment interchange at Miami.

The inauguration of Braniff's service over the newly-awarded 1,050-mile route segment between Texas points, the Mid-South, Washington and New York in February, 1956, culminated twelve years of effort by the airline to extend its domestic routes from the Southwest to the East Coast.

Initial step in a new flight equipment program was the purchase of seven Douglas DC-7C aircraft. Braniff's fleet of 62-passenger DC-7C "El Dorados" was placed

Junkers *F-13* was pioneer all-metal, low-wing monoplane in Lufthansa service.

in service on domestic routes in the fall of 1956, and in the spring of 1957 Braniff introduced "El Dorado" service over its international system between the U.S. and Latin America.

Another phase of the 1955 fleet expansion program was the purchase of nine Lockheed Electra turbo-prop aircraft at a cost of nearly 22 million dollars for the planes and spare equipment. First of the 75-passenger turbine-powered planes were delivered in May, 1959 and Braniff's Electra service was inaugurated June 15, 1959.

Also during 1955 the company announced the purchase of five Boeing 707-227 jet transports at a total cost of 30 million dollars for the planes, spare parts and engines. First of the 600 mile-an-hour, 106-passenger jets was placed in service on Texas-New York and Texas-Chicago schedules in December, 1959.

Five Convair 440 Metropolitan airliners, also a part of the new equipment program, were ordered during 1956 and delivery of the 44-passenger transports was completed during January, 1957.

Modification of Braniff's Douglas DC-6 fleet at a cost of $1,200,000 was completed in the company's shops during 1956 and 1957. More powerful engines, which increased the plane's speed to 325 miles-per-hour, were installed and the passenger cabin interiors were completely refurbished.

A major move to improve the airline's ground facilities came in June, 1955, when a long term agreement was signed with the City of Dallas for the construction and lease of a new multi-million dollar maintenance and overhaul base for the airline at Love Field. Construction was begun in March, 1957, and the new maintenance and operations facilities was occupied by Braniff in the fall of 1958.

Additional steps to improve the airline's ground facilities were taken in 1956, including the announcement of plans for a new ten-story Braniff Airways Building in Dallas. The airline's entire system-wide administrative offices occupied their new quarters in February, 1958.

Braniff placed a new electronic reservations control system in operation in February, 1958, thus becoming the first airline in the world to adopt such a program on a system-wide basis. The electronic unit, which is tied in with Braniff's entire communications system, keeps track of seats on all flights throughout the airline's complete system 31 days in advance and automatically notifies all Braniff stations and sales offices of seat availabilities.

In October, 1958, when the move into the airline's new multi-million dollar maintenance and operations base was begun, a new, completely automatic high-speed teletype network was placed in operation, linking more than 100 Braniff offices located in 51 cities on the airline's routes throughout the United States. The new system handles messages for all flight and ground operations, including weather advisories, as well as reservartions and general administrative messages of the airline. Braniff's electronic reservations control system was integrated with the new teletype network to give the airline the finest, most efficient means available of handling reservations.

The first commercial air service from the southwestern United States to Bogota, Colombia, was inaugurated by Braniff in January, 1960. Simultaneously, the airline began new non-stop flights from Texas to Panama on its Texas-Colombia schedules.

Other major improvements in Braniff's Latin American service also were effective during 1960. In April the airline placed its El Dorado Super Jets in service between the U.S. and Panama, Peru, Argentina and Brazil, and to Bogota, Columbia in July. Braniff's through jet schedules are operated from New York to South America via Miami under an interchange agreement with Eastern Air Lines.

The latest step in Braniff's fleet expansion program was announced in March, 1960 when the company's management gave Boeing Airplane company a letter of intent to purchase three Boeing 720-027 jet aircraft for delivery on each in February, April and August of 1961. A fourth was purchased in April, 1961 for delivery in May, 1962.

In May, 1961, a group of four of Dallas' business and civic leaders, J. Erik Jonsson, Eugene McDermott, Patrick Haggerty and Cecil Green, acquired all the shares of stock formerly owned by Senator William A. Blakley and the Blakley-Braniff Foundation, a total of more than a million shares.

Braniff currently is operating a fleet of 65 aircraft, including 7 Boeing El Dorado Super Jets, 8 Lockheed Electras, 6 DC-7C "El Dorados," 10 DC-6's, 6 Convair 440's, 25 Convair 340's, and three all cargo planes.

The airline's domestic routes extend from Chicago and Minneapolis-St. Paul through Kansas City and Oklahoma City south to New Orleans and such Texas cities as Dallas, Fort Worth, San Antonio, Houston and Brownsville. From New York and Washington, Braniff serves the Southwest via Memphis, Nashville and Chattanooga, Tennessee. Its western route terminates in Denver. Braniff's International routes presently serve the Latin American countries of Mexico, Cuba, Panama, Colombia, Ecuador, Peru, Bolivia, Paraguay, Argentina and Brazil.

Braniff's employees totaled approximately 5,800 at the end of 1960.

Many years after their introduction, *F-13's* were still active. This ski plane was used by Canadian Pacific in the far north.

HISTORY OF PLANES FLOWN by BRANIFF INTERNATIONAL AIRWAYS

Stinson-Detroiter: The name "Braniff" first appeared in the air transport industry on June 20, 1928, when a company, Paul R. Braniff, Inc., organized by Thomas E. Braniff and his younger brother, Paul, commenced operations as a scheduled airline between Oklahoma City and Tulsa, a distance of 116 air miles. This was the first passenger-carrying airline in the Southwest. The airplane used was a Stinson-Detroiter with six seats, one for the pilot and five for passengers. Its fuselage and wings were framed by steel tubing with wood catstrips between and covered by impregnated canvas, and the wings were supported by braces fastened to the bottom of the fuselage. The Stinson was powered by a single Wright "Whirlwind" 225 hp engine and had been purchased originally in 1927 for approximately $11,000 by the Braniff brothers and other associates for their own pleasure trips. Cruise speed of the Stinson was 105 miles per hour, fuel capacity was 50 gallons, and the plane had an allowable useful load of approximately 1,000 pounds.

The first Braniff plane was used over the original route, and an extension to Wichita Falls (early 1929), until the merger of Paul R. Braniff, Inc., with Universal Aviation Corporation in the summer of 1929.

Lockheed Vega: The present Braniff Airways was incorporated November 3, 1930 and ten days later, on November 13, 1930, commenced its first scheduled flights, carrying passengers and air express only, between Tulsa, Oklahoma City and Wichita Falls. Two new 6-passenger Lockheed Vegas were purchased at a cost of approximately $10,000 each. The Vegas had a wooden fuselage covered with impregnated fabric.

The small but speedy planes cruised at 150 miles per hour, had a fuel capacity of 90 gallons and could carry a payload of 1200 pounds. The Vega's single engine was a Pratt & Whitney 425 hp "Wasp".

Between November, 1930 and June, 1937, Braniff owned and operated a total of ten Vegas.

Ford Tri-Motor: In the fall of 1934, Braniff Airways acquired the Long and Harmon Air Service, which held mail contracts to serve ten Texas communities. Included in the flight equipment acquired were two Ford Tri-Motor airplanes. The all-metal planes, powered with Pratt & Whitney S1D1 500 hp engines, carried 14 passengers at a speed of 110 miles per hour. Fuel capacity was approximately 250 gallons, and the "Tin Goose" had a gross payload of nearly 4,000 pounds.

Braniff operated the Tri-Motors on the South Texas schedules until the summer of 1935 when they were replaced with 10-passenger Lockheed Electras.

Lockheed 10-A "Electra": Braniff Airways' first twin-engine aircraft was the Lockheed 10-A "Electra", all-metal monoplane. In January, 1935 Braniff purchased a fleet of seven Electras at a cost of $50,000 each. The first Electra was delivered in March and placed in service in April of that year.

The 10-passenger airplanes, powered by two Pratt & Whitney "Wasp Junior" 450 hp engines, had a fuel

capacity of 200 gallons and cruised at 160 miles an hour.

The Electras were used over Braniff's "Great Lakes to the Gulf" route until June, 1940.

Douglas DC-2: In March, 1937, Braniff ordered five Douglas DC-2s to supplement its Electra fleet. The first 14-passenger plane was delivered to Braniff in Oklahoma City two months later. Braniff made its inaugural DC-2 flights, which also featured the airline's first air hostess service, on June 12, 1937.

Powered by two Wright "Cyclone" 750 hp engines, the DC-2 cruised at 165 miles an hour. Fuel capacity was 660 gallons, and the gross payload of the airplane was approximately 3,300 pounds.

Douglas DC-3: In August, 1939, Braniff announced the purchase of four new 21-passenger Douglas DC-3 airliners at a cost of approximately $100,000 each. The first "Super B-Liner" was received by the airline in December, 1939 and went into regular scheduled service between Dallas and Amarillo in February, 1940. Four more were ordered in March, 1940, and an additional three DC-3s were delivered in May, 1941.

Braniff's twin-engine DC-3s, powered with Wright "Cyclone" 1100 hp engines, cruised at 180 miles an hour with a top speed of 212 mph. The airliner carried 800 gallons of fuel and had an allowable useful load of 4,900 pounds.

Throughout the next decade, Braniff added to its fleet of DC-3 aircraft and by August, 1952, when Braniff and Mid-Continent Airlines merged, the combined airlines operated a total of 34 DC-3s. Braniff retired its DC-3s from scheduled service in April, 1960.

Lockheed Lodestar: The twin-engine 14-passenger Lockheed Lodestar was operated throughout the Upper Midwest between September, 1940 and May, 1946 by Mid-Continent Airlines, now a part of Braniff Airways. The two carriers merged in August, 1952.

Considered the fastest commercial aircraft in the air at the time, the Lodestar cruised at 200 miles an hour, with a maximum cruise speed of 240 miles per hour. It was powered with two Pratt & Whitney 885 hp S1E3G "Hornet" engines, had a fuel capacity of 644 gallons and an allowable useful load of 6,330 pounds.

Douglas DC-4: Braniff acquired its first four-engine aircraft shortly after the close of World War II when it purchased from the government five C-54 military aircraft for conversion to passenger airliners. The first DC-4 flights were inaugurated between Texas points, Kansas City and Chicago in May, 1946. Five additional DC-4s were purchased in June, 1946 and the airplanes were used on the airline's domestic and international routes until October, 1953.

The 46-passenger planes cruised at 210 miles per hour and had a 3,000-gallon fuel capacity. The DC-4s were powered with Pratt & Whitney 1450 hp "Twin Wasp" engines and had an allowable payload of 13,000 pounds.

French Potez 32 Served Air France in early days, had capacity of four, cruised at 102 mph.

Douglas DC-6: In May, 1946, Braniff was granted 7,719 miles of international routes to Cuba, Panama and South America and the following month placed an order with Douglas Aircraft Company for six 52-passenger DC-6 aircraft. First of the new $700,000 airliners was delivered to Braniff in August, 1947 and began service over the Texas-Chicago route in November of that year. Service on the international routes was inaugurated in June, 1948 with the DC-6s.

Initially powered with four Pratt & Whitney R-2800 CA-15 engines of 2100 hp each, the DC-6 cruised at 275 miles per hour with a fuel capacity of 4,248 gallons and an allowable payload of 15,515 pounds. During 1956 Braniff's DC-6 fleet was modified and the power plants converted to the Pratt & Whitney R-2800-CB-16 engines, increasing the cruising speed to 325 miles an hour.

Convair 340: Braniff was the first airline in the world to offer scheduled air service with the 44-passenger Convair 340 aircraft. The $600,000 airliners were placed in service over Braniff's domestic routes on November 1, 1952.

Powered with two 2400 hp Pratt & Whitney R-2800-CB-16 engines, the Convair 340 has a normal cruise speed of 275 miles an hour, a fuel capacity of 1,730 gallons and an allowable useful load of 13,774 pounds.

The airline's fleet currently includes 25 of the Convair 340s and six of the later model Convair 440 which have been in service since December, 1956.

Lockheed L-049 Constellation: To supplement its fleet of four-engine aircraft, Braniff purchased two Lockheed Constellations which were used on domestic schedules from September, 1955 until September, 1959.

The 54-passenger planes cruised at 290 miles per hour and had a fuel capacity of 4,690 gallons. Powered with four 2200 hp Wright R-3350-BA-3 engines, the Constellation had a gross payload of 19,891 pounds.

Douglas DC-7C: The long-range Douglas DC-7C has been a part of the Braniff fleet since October, 1956 and the airline currently operates six of the 66-passenger planes in both domestic and international service. Powered with four Wright R-3350 compound engines with 3400 hp each, the DC-7C cruises at 360 miles per hour and has an allowable useful load of 24,071 pounds. With a fuel capacity of 7,824 gallons, the DC-7C has an operational non-stop flight range of more than 5,000 miles.

Each DC-7C aircraft cost approximately $2,600,000.

Lockheed L-188 Electra: First turbo-prop aircraft to join the Braniff fleet was the Lockheed L-188, which was placed in service by the airline in June, 1959. The 68-passenger Electras are used on Braniff's domestic routes and on schedules between the United States and Mexico City. With a fuel capacity of 5,520 gallons, the Electra cruises at 410 miles an hour and has a payload capacity of 26,957 pounds. It is powered with four 3750 hp Allison 501 turbo engines.

Braniff currently operates eight of the $2,500,000 aircraft.

Boeing 707-227: Service with the world's fastest jetliners was inaugurated by Braniff in December, 1959, and four of the $5,500,000 pure jet aircraft currently are in use over the airline's domestic and international system.

The Braniff 707s are powered with four Pratt & Whitney Jt4A-3 engines, each developing 15,800 pounds of thrust at takeoff. With a cruising speed of 606 miles per hour and a fuel capacity of 15,456 gallons, Braniff's Super Jets have a cruising range of 3,500 miles. The big jetliner has a payload capacity of 52,057 pounds.

Single engined Fokker utilized by Swissair for short hops presaged trimotor.

33

Bleriot 27 was built for Air France by one of earliest aviation companies, carried six in porthole-windowed cabin.

Curtiss *Kingbird* was twin engined Eastern Airlines transport which cruised at 110 mph.

Three engines were obviously the answer, no matter how they were mounted, as witness this Koolhoven FK-33 flying over Amsterdam.

Handley Page *Trimotor* carried ten passengers at a time for Sabena, Belgian airline.

CANADIAN PACIFIC AIRLINES

THE GROWTH of Canadian Pacific Airlines to global proportions since its beginnings as a scattered group of small "bush" operations in northern Canada, has been one of the marvels of modern transportation.

Formed in 1942 by the amalgamation of 10 independent air services in western and northern Canada, the Airline today operates a 44,700-mile route pattern linking five continents as well as major cities in Canada. This pattern comprises 7,500 domestic route miles (including 2,450 miles on the mainline service inaugurated on May 4, 1959).

The overseas routes, 37,200 miles in extent, stretch from Hong Kong through Tokyo, Vancouver, Mexico City, Lima and Santiago, to Buenos Aires; from Australia and New Zealand to Fiji, through Honolulu and Vancouver, thence over the Polar Route to Amsterdam and Rome; and from Mexico City through Toronto and Montreal to Lisbon, Madrid, and Rome. In August, 1961, the Honorable Leon Balcer, Canada's Minister of Transport, announced the Federal Cabinet's decision granting CPA traffic rights into London on the Polar Route. The Federal Cabinet announcement also granted CPA traffic rights out of Calgary and Edmonton on the Vancouver-London Route, along with a technical stop at Gander, as required under the terms of the Canada/United Kingdom Bilateral Air Agreement.

Canadian Pacific has become renowned as "The World's Greatest Travel System" and continues to maintain leadership in the operation of steamships, hotels, telegraphs, express services, highway transport and other facilities. Canadian Pacific demonstrated its interest in aviation as early as 1919 when the Company obtained a special permit from the Canadian Government to own and operate commercial aircraft.

It was not until 1933, however, that the Company became directly interested in large-scale air operations when it paid $50,000 for a block of stock in Canadian Airways, which then operated in the northwestern areas of Canada.

During the thirties, the Canadian bush pilots had pioneered a network of northern air routes linking isolated communities and potentially rich mining areas with the end of steel. By the end of that decade, however, the numerous small bush companies were in serious difficulties because of inadequate finances, rising costs, and the use of small, inefficient aircraft.

It was under these circumstances that Canadian Pacific undertook the task of organizing northern air transportation into a co-ordinated pattern.

Meanwhile, at the time of the fall of France, in June, 1940, the British Government asked Canadian Pacific to assist in organizing a service to ferry bombers over the Atlantic. Canadian Pacific organized and directed this service through its formative period, after which it was taken over by the Royal Air Force.

Another major aviation contribution by Canadian Pacific was the Airline's operation of six air observer schools on a non-profit basis during the war, as part of the British Commonwealth Air Training Plan.

In line with Canada's stepped-up national defense effort, CPA was commissioned to operate The Royal Canadian Air Force No. 10 Repair Station at Calgary on June 15, 1951. Work at this depot, which still continues, is largely maintenance on all types of military aircraft.

CPA played a prominent part in Canada's contribution to the United Nations during the Korean campaign. Following the inception of the airlift in 1950, the Airline made 703 return trips over the 4,800-mile route between Vancouver and Tokyo.

Passengers carried included both Canadian and American personnel totalling 39,313 and the Company's planes logged over 7,000,000 miles on the Great Circle Route via the Aleutian Islands.

Domestic Lines

In its domestic operations, CPA now carries modern pioneers and their equipment to and from North America's last frontiers, Alaska and the Yukon. Into a land formerly accessible only by dog sled and river boat, CPA now operates a year-round scheduled passenger and freight service.

In one of the most dramatic barters in Canadian airline history, CPA traded its Ontario and Quebec domestic routes for Trans-Canada Airline's Toronto to Mexico run. The exchange took place in September, 1955, and CPA inaugurated its non-stop Toronto-to-Mexico service on November 6th of the same year. This route continues southward to Lima, Peru, Santiago, Chile, and Buenos Aires, Argentina, and was later extended eastward to Montreal, Lisbon, Madrid and Rome.

The most significant development in the history of Canadian commercial aviation since the formation of CPA in 1942, took place on May 4, 1959, with the inauguration of the Airline's "Canadian Empress" service. CPA's Britannias established a new transcontinental service which offered the fastest flights in Canada between Vancouver, Winnipeg, Toronto and Montreal. This service, consisting of one flight a day in each direction, afforded tourist class passengers the luxury of jet-powered flight for the first time in Canada. Six-hundred-mile-an-hour DC-8 jetliners have replaced the Britannias on the transcontinental service.

The Canadian Air Transport Board conducted a hearing in Edmonton on June 16, 1959, to determine the destiny of CPA's MacKenzie District — comprising the Company's routes stretching from Edmonton to the shores of the Arctic Ocean. In keeping with its policy of providing expansion opportunities for smaller airlines, while seeking to standardize equipment and extend its own mainline-type services, CPA made application to relinquish the MacKenzie, and Pacific Western Airlines applied for the right to operate these services. Pacific Western Airlines completed taking over the operation on July 20, 1959.

Overseas Lines

From Vancouver's International Airport, Canadian Pacific Airlines now operates its fast-expanding international services.

Fokker F-7 was first in series of pace-setting Fokker tri-motored craft.

In addition to many communities in Canada, CPA serves Tokyo and Hong Kong; Sydney, Auckland, Fiji and Honolulu; Mexico City, Lima, Santiago, and Buenos Aires; Amsterdam, via the Polar Route; Santa Maria, Lisbon, Madrid and Rome. CPA is one of the few airlines in the world which flies over the International Dateline, the Equator and the Arctic Circle.

Canadian Pacific Airlines is flying into the jet age at full throttle. The Company is now operating a fleet of DC-8 jetliners on its major overseas routes plus its Canadian transcontinental service. The Super DC-8, powered by the new Rolls-Royce Conway engines, is the most powerful commercial jet aircraft in the world. In addition, the Company has a fleet of Bristol Britannia jet-prop airliners which re-inforce DC-8 service on the Company's international route pattern.

CPA inaugurated its first overseas route to Australia in July, 1949. During the flight, both the Equator and the International Dateline are crossed. Stops are made enroute at Honolulu, Fiji, and Auckland.

On the Orient run, which was inaugurated, September, 1949, Britannias head westward via the Aleutians and cross the International Dateline to cover nearly 5,000 miles before touching down at Tokyo, and another 2,000 miles to reach Hong Kong.

In October, 1953, service between Vancouver, Mexico City and Lima, Peru began. This linked up with the North Pacific service to provide a one-carrier flight from Hong Kong to South America. Permission was received in May, 1956, from Argentina, to extend this route into Buenos Aires from Lima, and in September, 1957, a service connecting Lima, Santiago, Chile and Buenos Aires was inaugurated.

In June, 1955, in the face of widespread skepticism, CPA took what some writers termed a "million dollar gamble" by pioneering a Polar Route between Vancouver and Amsterdam, Holland. However, because of the route's popularity, it now includes a regular traffic stop at Edmonton whereby the Airline taps the vast passenger potential of the Prairie Provinces. The Polar flights from Vancouver are linked directly with the South Pacific service, to form one of the longest airline routes in the world.

On March 4, 1960, the Airline extended service from Lisbon to Rome to establish the first Canadian air link to the Eternal City. This development was followed by the Canadian Government's announcement regarding CPA's service linking western Canada and the United Kingdom on August 15, 1961.

Facilities

To handle the operation of these extensive services, Canadian Pacific has established its headquarters at Vancouver International Airport in the former Boeing Aircraft Company's hangar and buildings which CPA purchased from the War Assets Corporation. As a part of the Company's $20,000,000 jet age expansion program, headquarters facilities have been expanded to include a $1,400,00 hangar, largest of its kind in Canadian civil aviation, to house and service turbine-powered transports. A new, modern office building, nerve centre for the Airline's domestic and overseas operations, has been constructed on the Sea Island site. The executive, administrative, operational and maintenance work of the Company is carried out at Vancouver headquarters by a staff of over 2000 employees. A flight simulator building has been completed to house both a Britannia and DC-6B simulator for crew training.

Officers

Heading the organization is G. W. Grant McConachie, President, who played a major role in the development of North Country flying during the 1930's and in 1945 won the McKee Trophy for "Long and Outstanding Service in the Field of Aviation" in Canada.

F-7B was used by Swissair. Capacity: Ten passengers; cruising speed: 111 mph.

41

KLM bought Fokker *F-9* tri-motors for East Indian route, surveyed in 1927.

Pan American Airways took Fokker F-10's to Caribbean and South America, employed them for many years.

Famous Ford *Trimotor*, called the 'Tin Goose' by veteran pilots went everywhere.

Northwest Ford *Trimotor* hauled fifteen passengers at 110 mph along Great Lake route.

CONTINENTAL AIRLINES

A SMALL regional carrier just a few years ago, Continental Air Lines today is one of the nation's leading jet operators. The company has almost 3,000 employees headed by Robert F. Six, who has been president for the past 24 years.

In its 28-year history, Continental has flown 10 million passengers, 5 billion revenue passenger miles. This year, the company will fly approximately 1.5 million passengers, 1 billion revenue passenger miles.

Continental began operations on July 15, 1934, as the Southwest Division of Varney Speed Lines, flying a 520-mile route between Pueblo, Colo., Albuquerque, N. M., and El Paso, Tex. The company carried nine passengers in the first 15 days of operation. Today, Continental serves 36 cities on a 7,000-mile route through nine states, flying between Los Angeles, Denver, Kansas City and Chicago; between Los Angeles, Arizona and Texas; throughout the Rocky Mountain region and the Southwest.

Four Golden Jet Boeing 707s, four Golden Jet Boeing 720Bs and 12 jet-powered Viscount IIs account for 97 per cent of the company's daily seat miles — the highest percentage of jet-powered service offered by any trunkline in the nation.

The Golden Jets are maintained at Continental's multi-million-dollar jet maintenance base in Los Angeles; the jet-powered Viscount IIs at Denver. The company's hostess training school is located at Los Angeles International Airport.

From its small beginning in 1934, Continental slowly grew into a regional carrier, then into a major trunkline.

In 1937, Varney purchased the Denver-Pueblo route of Wyoming Air Service; later the same year changed the corporate name to Continental Air Lines, Inc.

Through a series of awards from the Civil Aeronautics Board beginning in 1939, Continental's basic Denver-El Paso route was extended from Denver to Wichita, Tulsa, and Kansas City; from El Paso to San Antonio and Kansas City. Extension from San Antonio to Houston was granted in 1951 to permit operation of interchange service of Continental and American Airlines between Houston, San Antonio and the West Coast via El Paso.

The next year, Continental began interchange service with Mid-Continent Air Lines (now part of Braniff International Airways) between Denver and St. Louis via Kansas City; in 1953 began interchange service with United Air Lines between Tulsa, Wichita and Seattle via Denver.

In April, 1955, absorption of the routes and operations of Pioneer Air Lines added Dallas/Ft. Worth, Austin, and other cities in Texas and New Mexico to Continental's system.

In November, 1955, the Civil Aeronautics Board certificated Continental to begin service between Chicago and Los Angeles, via Denver and Kansas City, turning the company into a major trunk carrier. Service began over the route in 1957.

In April, 1959, Continental began flying over its newly awarded nonstop routes linking Dallas/Ft. Worth with El Paso, Albuquerque, Lubbock, Midland/Odessa and Amarillo.

In June, 1961, Continental inaugurated nonstop flights between Houston and Los Angeles and via San Antonio, El Paso, Phoenix and Tucson.

Continental still has a number of major route applications pending before the Civil Aeronauticcs Board, including requests to fly between the Mainland and Hawaii; to fly nonstop between Dallas/Ft. Worth and both Houston and San Antonio; to fly nonstop between major cities in Texas, Oklahoma and Colorado; and to extend the company's system into the East by flying over a Chicago-Cleveland-New York route and between Cleveland and Philadelphia.

To supplement its present equipment, Continental technical teams are studying all short-range jet transports. A special team also is concentrating on supersonic transports, which the company believes will be flying in scheduled airline service by 1970.

Eastern Airlines carried both passengers and cargo in fleet of Fords which were all metal in contrast to Fokker plywood construction.

Up-dated and modernized Ford *Trimotor* was one of the last to go into service. Many of these sturdy craft are still flying in remote areas.

Fokker Trimotor series continued with F-12, here in service of KLM, Royal Dutch Airline.

F-18 was capable of 143 mph cruising speed, had fourteen-passenger capacity.

Looking like a prehistoric monster, this Junkers JU-38 settles in at a Berlin airport with thirty passengers aboard.

United Airlines flew Boeing 80-A trimotor biplanes on Chicago-San Francisco run in 1929. Cruising at 115-120 mph, the 80-A seated nineteen.

EASTERN AIR LINES

EASTERN AIR LINES in 1962 carried nearly 9 million passengers a total of more than 4¾ billion passenger miles, and had total operating revenues of over $291 million.

Under the leadership of Captain Eddie Rickenbacker, its Chairman of the Board and Malcolm A. MacIntyre, President and Chief Executive Officer, Eastern today has some 17,500 employees and 19,434 miles of routes linking 119 cities in 27 of the United States, plus parts of Canada, Mexico, Puerto Rico and Bermuda, and is still growing as the air transport industry moves rapidly ahead in the jet age.

During 1959 40 Lockheed Prop-Jet Electras were placed in service; in 1960 the first units of a fleet of some 15 pure-jet Douglas DC-8s joined the Eastern fleet, and by the Fall of 1961 the initial jet-age expansion program begun in 1957, had been completed as the second phase; involving acquisition of 15 Boeing-type 720 medium/long range jets and 40 Boeing/type 727 short range jets was getting under way.

Eastern's growth from 792 miles of routes, 44 employees, and a fleet of eight open-cockpit airplanes, has been phenomenal, but there are still many men in the company who remember the first operations — and some have hardly begun to turn grey.

Eastern started on May 1, 1928 when five airmen took off at night in tiny 200 horsepower, Mailwing aircraft with a determination to fly 300 pounds of mail each between New York and Atlanta.

Events leading up to the birth of the country's most successful airline on that date are a saga of American Enterprise — spelled with a capital "E".

It all began back in 1926 when the U.S. Government hopefully invited competitive bids for contracts to transport mail between New York (using Hadley Field, New Brunswick, N. J.) and Atlanta. There was no such thing as an "airway". No beacons, no radio stations, in fact in most places en route, no landing field.

Started By Harold Pitcairn

A young flier, Harold F. Pitcairn, who manufactured aircraft for county fair exhibits and owned a landing field near Philadelphia, wishfully filed a bid to carry mail at $3 per pound. Once his bid was accepted, Pitcairn first had to build an airplane to fulfill his contract.

There were other difficulties facing the enterprise in addition to the fact that the agreement was to deliver mail with planes that didn't exist to air fields that didn't exist. To have any advantage over railroads, air mail had to fly at night. Then the airplane's advantage of speed was so slight that they were still experimenting with methods of transferring mail from plane-to-train en route.

No Navigation Facilities

There were few cross-country fliers that would have any part of night trips — or flights through anything but the best of weather. Dash boards were adorned with eight, sometimes reliable instruments, including a compass, an oil gauge, a tachometer, and an altimeter.

"Blind" flying was strictly a stunt and "instrument" flying was still a dream in the laboratories of the Sperry Company. Navigation consisted of finding a railroad track and flying over it until you reached your destination.

But Pitcairn, seeing a market for both his planes and his talents in mail contracts, was undaunted. He bet that if he could just get the operation started, the refinements would come later — and won. He went ahead with the production of his planes, recruited a handful of World War I flying veterans and daredevil barnstormers, and began a survey of the routes.

Expansion Before Inauguration

He had the distinction of nearly doubling his operation before it even began.

In November, 1927, before he had ever hefted the first air mail sack, the government awarded Pitcairn Aviation this 595-mile route linking Atlanta with Miami. Thus Pitcairn found himself in possession of the "Eastern Air Lines" a total of 1387 air miles from New York to Miami.

Pitcairn had come through with an airplane to meet contract requirements, but inauguration of schedules was pushed ahead several times awaiting completion of the installation of airway beacons. Pilots whiled away their time, giving free flight instructions to gas boys and mechanics, practising their own flying techniques, and making local sightseeing trips.

Demand Double Schedules

Finally in late April the airways work was complete and it looked like the service would definitely start on the first of May. Much to everyone's surprise, the volume of first flight mail that accumulated before takeoff necessitated operation of double schedules. Two northbound flights took off from Atlanta, another from Greensboro, and two southbound schedules originated in the New York area.

At every stop en route pilots of these first flights were astounded to find citizenry by the hundreds swarming over the fields to welcome the new mail service.

Considering the problems and difficulties facing the young company, Pitcairn Aviation didn't turn in a bad record for the remaining eight months in 1928. In August air mail rates were reduced from 10 cents a half ounce to five cents for the first ounce and ten cents for each additional ounce, and double schedules became the rule rather than the exception. On December 1, Pitcairn began service over the Atlanta-Miami route, thus completing the "Eastern Air Lines".

First Operation Big Success

The company grew from 44 employees to 91 and the monthly payroll averaged $16,000. The tiny Mailwings flew 338,532 revenue miles and met 93% of their schedules. They carried 111,428 pounds of air mail. Of course, this is less than the amount Eastern carries in two days now, but then it would be hardly

First Curtiss Condor used liquid-cooled Curtiss Conqueror engines, carried twenty one passengers at 120 mph cruising.

"cricket" to compare today's vast organization with that embryonic operation.

With the airline launched and plenty of room for expansion, the future looked rosy — but only for a short while. There was plenty of turbulent weather ahead, and most of it had to do with finances.

Airline Sold To North American

After a full year's stab at running both a manufacturing and operating company, Pitcairn, who had become interested in a new aviation development, the autogiro, decided that his future was in building, rather than flying planes. On July 10, 1929, less than four months ahead of the Stock Market crash, he sold his airline to North American Aviation, Inc. for $2,500,000.

If it had not been absorbed by North American the airline would have probably folded during the depression years, because there was no "black ink" used in its books between 1931 and 1935. However, Pitcairn Aviation (whose name was soon changed to Eastern Air Transport) was just a Shetland Pony in the North American stable. In addition, the holding company owned a portion of the United Aircraft and Transport Corp., (later United Air Lines), Transcontinental Air Transport (later Trans-World Airlines) and a large group of aircraft manufacturing, sales, and service companies, then in the process of being merged into the Curtiss-Wright Corporation.

Expanded During Depression

Like motion pictures and the radio industry, commercial aviation was expanding and achieving its place in our way of life during the darkest days of the depression. Although Eastern lost money and needed an annual transfusion of funds from its parent company, it spread its wings more and more and showed "promise".

Passenger service was inaugurated and the company began a "collection" of transport aircraft including Curtiss Kingbirds, Ford Tri-motors, Stinsons, and Curtiss Condors. The operating base was moved from Richmond to the more centrally located Atlanta. Routes of another small airline were purchased and added to Eastern Air Transport. Formal pilot training to qualify airmen for instrument flying was adopted. Hostesses were added to crews.

Slowly but surely all of these moves were improving service and adding to the line's prestige and public acceptance.

Rickenbacker Returns To Aviation

In 1933 control of North American and all of its subsidiaries passed to General Motors Corp. Out of this transaction came a development which was to have more bearing on the future of Eastern than any since its inception.

Captain Eddie Rickenbacker joined North American Aviation.

At the time, Rickenbacker was making the difficult transistion from hero to industrialist. He had already carved his niche in the Hall of Fame, first as one of the country's leading automobile race drivers, then as the Ace of Aces in World War I with a record of 21 enemy airplanes and four balloons destroyed in aerial combat.

After his return to the United States and the traditional hero's ticker tape parade welcome, he had returned to his first love — automobiles. The initial venture, a car bearing his name, resulted in failure, primarily because it was too far advanced for its time. He jolted the established manufacturers by incorporating such unheard-of features as four-wheel brakes — which all declared were dangerous.

Pulling himself together after this misadventure, Rickenbacker had joined General Motors and assigned himself the task (although he was not legally responsible) of paying off the debts of the Rickenbacker Motor Car Company left when it went under.

Air Mail Contracts Cancelled

Captain Eddie had hardly begun to feel his way around in North American and the commercial aviation industry before all the airlines were struck a body blow in the early part of 1934. The Postmaster General issued an order cancelling all air mail contracts and mail delivery was turned over to the Army Air Force.

Twelve courageous, but woefully inexperienced, Army fliers lost their lives before this dark chapter in aviation history was closed. This was a terrific price to pay, but out of the experience came a national realization of the importance of the commercial airlines and also a revision and improvement in military flight training methods.

After the Government turned the mail operation back to the commercial lines, new air patterns were set up and a system which formed the nucleus of the present networks, was laid out. North American formed a new corporation, Eastern Air Lines, Inc. to bid for routes. Eastern was extended from Chicago to Atlanta and from Atlanta to New Orleans. Eastern once again moved its operating base, this time from Atlanta to Miami where it has remained ever since.

Rickenbacker Takes Over As Manager

Despite expansion, Eastern continued to lose money. At the request of General Motors, North American Aviation made Captain Rickenbacker a Vice President and General Manager of Eastern.

This "promotion" saddled Rickenbacker with probably the toughest assignment he will ever draw in his lifetime. Eastern was the "ugly duckling" of the entire air transport industry.

Its patchwork fleet included everything from some of the original Mailwings to a conglomeration of passenger and mail planes including Curtiss Condors, Kingbirds, and Stinsons. The 500-odd employees year after year had seen their efforts result in financial losses. They had reached a point where the morale curve was headed downhill. North American which had bought the line for $2,500,000 and in five years put twice that much more into it, was willing to sell out for an even $1,000,000 — but there were no takers.

When Rickenbacker took over, things began to happen — fast. During a whirlwind trip over every mile of the routes and into every office, he got acquainted with every employee. He talked over the problems. He promised these discouraged — but desperately hoping men and women — that he'd go to bat for them if they'd

Development of Condor was radial, air-cooled engined version, here in service of Eastern Airlines.

match his efforts and enthusiasm with loyalty and hard work.

His first move was to get rid of the obsolete aircraft that were eating the company out of house and home and replace them with new Douglas DC-2's, and subsequently their refined sister ships, the world-famous DC-3's.

He cut out the "frills" in flying and slapped on a rigid system of cost controls.

Eastern Begins To Make Money

In a year's time he convinced North American and General Motors that Eastern Air Lines could make money. The 1934 loss of $700,000 was converted to a $90,000 profit for 1935.

Each year thereafter definitive positive financial progress was made, but it was slow and painful. Captain Rickenbacker made recommendation after recommendation for what were then considered bold steps for expansion. But North American's attitude was wary and the management was willing to settle for just a little improvement at a time.

In 1936 Eastern netted $168,000, and $197,000 in 1937.

Then, once again, the boom was lowered!

G M Sells Eastern

This time General Motors decided to abandon its operating company in favor of its manufacturing interests. With war clouds forming, the doubtful airline was dropped so the corporation could concentrate on the lucrative rearmament program.

Although no one really wanted Eastern as an airline, it did appeal to some big corporations and banking houses as a piece of some bigger corporate deal. But with three years under Rickenbacker's stewardship, the sale price had gone up. One company made an irresistible bid of $3,250,000.

By now Rickenbacker was head of a cohesive group of men and women who called themselves the "Eastern Air Lines' Family". He was determined to save the airline for them — the people who had built it.

Captain Gets Into "Bidding"

He heard of the offer to buy the airline from a newspaper friend in the middle of the night. In typical Rickenbacker fashion he went right over to an old friend, Alfred P. Sloan, and got him out of bed.

The General Motors Chairman agreed that Captain Eddie's bid for the airline would be given equal consideration with all others.

In a thrilling photo-finish scramble, Rickenbacker, with the aid of friends in Smith, Barney & Co., and Kuhn, Loeb & Co., managed to outbid some powerful financial interests and make good on his promise to "save the company for the boys and girls that built it".

What happened after that is modern history and fairly common knowledge. Through application of loyalty, initiative, and plenty of hard work, Eastern became the basic air transport system for more than half of the United States. One of the "Big Four" of commercial aviation, Eastern is serving a great area reaching from New England and the Great Lakes in the North to Florida and the Gulf States in the South, from the Atlantic Seaboard and Puerto Rico on the East, to the Mississippi and Mid-Texas in the West.

World War II Service

During World War II, Eastern released half its fleet to the Military Services and had some 1200 employees in uniform. Although it ranged to such faraway fronts as Alaska, the company's main contribution to the War effort was the formation and operation of a route extending from Miami to Brazil and across the South Atlantic to Africa. Between 1942 and 1945 Eastern's military transport Division flew 60 million pounds of war material and 125,000 passengers to war theaters.

Colonial Airlines Merged

Eastern Air Lines acquired the assets of Colonial Airlines on June 1, 1956, marking another historic step in the ever expanding airline. With the merger making Colonial a division of Eastern Air Lines, it gave Eastern a total of 15,967 unduplicated route miles, linking Washington and New York with Montreal and Ottawa, Canada, as well as Bermuda, and stretching Eastern's network through 25 states from Chicago and New York to Texas, Florida and Puerto Rico. It added 800 Colonial employees to Eastern's then 13,500.

Mexican Link Added

Another major post-War objective was reached by Eastern in 1957 when it was finally, after 11 years of waiting, able to inaugurate flights between New York/Washington, New Orleans and Mexico City, thus linking for the first time by one air carrier the three capital cities of the North American Continent.

But growth does not end there. Eastern now seeks from the CAB authority to establish a single-carrier Southern Transcontinental Route linking Florida to California via the Gulf States.

Modernizing The Fleet

To effect an orderly transistion to revolutionary jet-powered operations, Eastern is currently embarked on a $422 million fleet expansion program, the largest ever undertaken by an individual airline.

Patterned to increase the total Eastern Air Lines fleet to 241 modern airliners, the program will triple the air carrier's passenger capacity by 1961. This "blueprint" to raise passenger speed "just under the sound barrier" has three distinct stages:

Golden And Silver Falcons

1. Acquisition of a fleet of 75 of the latest and fastest piston-driven pressurized airliners to meet increased traffic demands and the requirements of the expanded route networks following the combination of Colonial and Eastern.

This stage actually got underway in the fall of 1955 with the delivery of the first units of Eastern's now famous "Golden Falcon" fleet. Widely acclaimed everywhere it has been introduced as the "last word" in luxury, the Golden Falcon features cabin interiors and decor designed especially for Eastern Air Lines by Harley Earl, famed head of the General Motors design and styling staff. Public acceptance has been so enthusiastic that Eastern has already decided to employ the same materials and styling in its forthcoming "propjet" Electra airliners.

With Wright Cyclone radials, the Condor was 40 mph faster, had more capacity.

Completed in 1958, Eastern's piston-driven airliner program represents a total of 60 of these four-engine Golden Falcon transports.

To improve the service at intermediate cities in the Northern Division of its network, Eastern introduced 15 modern Convair Model 440 twin-engine transports known as "Silver Falcons". Carrying 44 passengers and cruising at upwards of 290 miles per hour, these airliners enabled Eastern to retire its smaller and slower DC-3's and DC-4's.

Prop-Jet Electras

2. Purchase of an initial fleet of 40 Lockheed "Electra" prop-jets, the first jet-powered commercial transport to go into production in the United States, at a cost of $100 million.

The selection of the "Electra" was made only after several years of study of jet-powered aircraft designs, including not only proposed U.S. plans, but first-hand analysis of several foreign models.

Measured to Eastern's requirements all available designs proved to be either too slow, too small, uneconomical or lacked suitable engines.

After rejecting all designs, Eastern developed its own specifications for the guidance of U.S. manufacturers. The result was the Electra which has now been adopted by other airlines.

Carrying 68 passengers in first-class service, the Electra moved transport speeds up into the 400-plus miles per hour range, and introduced a number of innovations, not only in speed, but in luxury, passenger comfort, convenience and quietness.

The first Electra went into scheduled service on Jan. 12, 1959, and the entire fleet was delivered during the year. This fleet increased the airline's airlift capacity to nearly 10 billion seat miles. Subsequently modified and improved into what is now called the "Super Electra", this prop-jet has established itself as the "work horse" of the airline industry, and well lived up to the prediction that it would introduce the jet age to more people and more communities than any other type of aircraft.

Coming Of The DC-8s

3. Finally, to usher in the true jet age, Eastern ordered a $108 million fleet of 16 great Douglas DC-8 straight jet airliners equipped with larger, faster Pratt & Whitney J-75 engines which can fly 40-50 m.p.h. faster than earlier model jet transports without use of water injection.

Eastern selected the Douglas DC-8, first, because it was a pure commercial transport design from its inception and, therefore, not limited by basic military requirements. Second, the Douglas organization could devote to its successful development the full design and manufacturing resources in high speed aircraft and its wealth of experience gained through literally millions of hours logged by the distinguished series of DC commercial aircraft.

The first DC-8 was delivered to Eastern early in 1960, and by late 1961 all 15 will be received.

With the DC-8's in operation, Eastern was able to cut in half the travel time between some of the most widely separated points on its routes in the eastern half of the United States, Canada, Mexico, Bermuda and Puerto Rico. During 1961 jet service was being provided at New York, Chicago, Philadelphia, Boston, Atlanta, Miami, Houston, New Orleans, Tampa, San Juan, Montreal, Mexico City, and Bermuda.

MacIntyre Joins Eastern Family

On October 1, 1959, Captain Eddie Rickenbacker, who had held the top executive authority in Eastern Air Lines ever since the organization of the present company in 1938, passed on the title of Chief Executive Officer to a new President, Malcolm A. MacIntyre, in a realignment of executive responsibilities for the jet age. Mr. MacIntyre had recently resigned as Under Secretary of the U.S. Air Force.

Among the major changes which he effected in the company were the institution of a new Customer Services Department, concerned primarily with the problems of the passenger from the moment he called in for a reservation, through his ticketing, actual flight, arrival at destination, and claiming of baggage. He also introduced the "Air-Bus" and "Air-Shuttle" concepts of frill-free transportation.

Along with improvements in the handling of reservations, ticketing, baggage, and meals in flight, great strides were taken in upgrading Eastern's on-time performance record. By May of 1961 Eastern was leading the industry in punctual arrivals, according to official figures compiled by the Civil Aeronautics Board.

"Second Generation" Jets

In 1960 Eastern placed $66 million orders for 15 medium/long range jets of the Boeing-type 720, 12 of which were scheduled to go into service on various North-South routes during the fall of 1961, with 3 more units to be delivered during the first months of 1962. These "second generation" jets, provide approximately the same passenger and cargo capacity as DC-8's, but operate more economically over shorter ranges. They are equipped with improved Pratt & Whitney JT-3 engines which, like the JT-4s used on the DC-8s, do not require water injection.

Also in 1960 Eastern ordered a $170 million fleet of Boeing-type 727 medium range jets for delivery beginning in 1963. These planes, which are of an unusual design, will be powered by three rear-mounted Pratt & Whitney by-pass engines enabling to reach high jet speeds on medium ranges without the necessity of attaining high altitude. These 720's will eventually replace propeller-driven equipment now in use.

Swissair Condor, was first in Europe to carry stewardess to care for twenty four passengers.

Fairchild *Pilgrim* was rare transport/mail plane used by American, cruised at 117.

Amphibians were used my many lines in 1920's and '30's. Air France CAMS 53 flew Mediterranean.

Pan American operated this Sikorsky S-36 in pioneering phase.

Northwest Sikorsky S-38B was used around Great Lakes for a number of years.

EL AL ISRAEL AIRLINES

ONE of the few subjects on which today's hardboiled airline executives will agree is the basic ingredients for a new international trunk carrier — plenty of hard currency, skilled maintenance men and air crews, good equipment and ample stocks of spare parts, experienced commercial management and a strong foreign office to get those vital traffic rights. This may explain the growing interest in one of the most extraordinary air transport developments in recent years, the growth of El Al Israel Airlines, chosen instrument of the historic land of miracles.

With very little in the way of either Yankee dollars or British pounds, less than fifty trained aircraft mechanics, a few U.S. Army Air Force war-surplus transports, small stocks of parts, a damaged airport headquarters, a scant half-dozen employees with any commercial airline experience, and a bold but busy diplomatic corps that was desperately maneuvering to ensure national survival, Israel has built an aggressive carrier which carries her flag across 12,000 miles and three continents. It was no miracle.

A Child of War

It was the result of a combination of national need, absolute determination, indifference to work and weather, a certain amount of useful ignorance and a healthy determination to learn. The story began long before the birth of the State of Israel, in the late thirties when far-seeing planners of the Jewish Confederation of Labor in Israel (Histadrut) and their brethren in the underground Jewish defense forces (Haganah) got together to set up a small flying school and charter company. This firm was named Aviron, and it trained pilots in single-engine planes by day while plans were moving ahead to build up an air arm for the secret army.

A de Havilland twin-engine Rapide was added shortly before the Second World War, and it ranged as far as London on charter jobs. Then the shortage of aviation gasoline and spare parts practically grounded the little flying service, and it was not until 1946 that Aviron could resume normal operations. Internal friction was growing rapidly in Palestine, and Aviron's small planes made many unreported flights with high officers of the Jewish underground.

The lessons of air power learned so bitterly in World War II were not lost upon the military advisers of the Jewish community, and as it became clear that open fighting would follow the withdrawal of British troops, the future leaders of Israel began to purchase fighters, bombers and transport aircraft. In a dozen secret transactions on both sides of the Atlantic, Spitfires and Messerschmitts, B-17's, DC-3's and DC-4's, and squat Curtiss Commandos were hastily bought. And there was a terrible need for them when the Mandatory soldiers left, for Arab Legion troops rolled towards the great airport at Lydda, and the thirteen foreign carriers who had been serving Palestine abruptly halted their services.

With hostile armies on three sides and the sea at their backs, the grim Israelis fashioned a slim lifeline of battered planes and ships to bring in the essential men and supplies. Much equipment came down from Czechoslovakia in big DC-4's and commodious C-46's, hundreds of tons of munitions and guns moving through the night on an air service which didn't officially exist. Transports owned by Panamanian corporations and flown by veteran American, British and South African pilots were filled with war surplus munitions at secret airfields south of Prague and flown through the Iron Curtain to camouflaged bases north of Tel Aviv. More men and material came from South African Zionists in the DC-3's of the new Universal Air Services.

Foundation and Founders

When the great base which the British had built at Lydda was finally recaptured by Israeli armored units, they found a shambles. What wasn't missing had been smashed to bits. But the big runways, the terminal buildings, and the hangar stood intact. Work was begun to restore the field to use, and the young Government decided in November of 1948 that Israel should have her own airline. The new country could not count on foreign carriers in another emergency.

El Al Israel Airlines was incorporated in Tel Aviv on November 15, 1948, with a share capital of 2,000,000 Israeli pounds. Control of basic policy goes with two £1,000 "Founder's Shares" which are held by the Government, and the Ministry of Finance has also purchased £607,000 of the £1,057,000 worth of ordinary shares issued thus far. The national steamship company Zim holds £250,000, and it is reported that these were paid for with a DC-4 instead of cash. The dominant trade union body called Histadrut, a moderate Socialist group which owns and operates some of the most important manufacturing, processing and agricultural combines in the adolescent state, owns £50,000 of stock.

El Al, which is often translated from Hebrew as "To the Skies!" or "Onwards and Upwards!," started scheduled operations to Paris in July 1949 with DC-4's based at the rebuilt Lydda Airport. Post-war traffic to the Holy Land has been good even before the birth of Israel, and now Zionists and sympathizers were interested in seeing this infant democracy. Other carriers resumed their operations to Lydda, and the high load factors pointed the directions in which the Israeli airline was to expand. By the end of 1950, three DC-4's and two C-46's were in use on regular flights to London, Paris, Zurich, Rome, Athens, Istanbul, and Nicosia. There were also scheduled services to New York and Johannesburg, the latter by way of Khartoum and Nairobi. It was in 1950 that El Al absorbed Universal, which had been running between South Africa and Israel with twin-engine Douglas equipment.

From Manager down to Assistant Mechanic

Another acquisition from South Africa was El Al Managing Director Louis A. Pincus, energetic Johannesburg K.C. who had made a name as an effective courtroom lawyer, a moving speaker, and head of the Union of South Africa branch of Prime Minister Ben Gurion's Mapai Party. He had no aviation experience when he

Sikorsky S-38B was ten passenger Amphibian which cruised at 110.

became Legal Adviser to the Israeli Ministry of Transport and Communications in 1949, but he learned quickly in the negotiations for bilateral air transport agreements with Britain and the United States. He has also played a key role in other treaties governing the exchange of landing rights, and is undoubtedly the strongest voice in the discussions of Israel's air policy. Pincus took the top job at El Al in 1950; he has driven himself and his colleagues unceasingly during the past three years. There can be no question that he is the boss of the civil aviation program of the young democracy. A shrewd, charming, practical man, he has the burden of finding or training assistants who can handle many of the details of the Israeli air transport program.

Working closely with Pincus are Deputy Managing Director Yoel Palgi, an ex-paratrooper and author whose imaginative mind frequently aids with planning; Vice-President (commercial affairs) Abraham Rywkind, a tough lawyer with business experience; Legal Adviser Lionel "Bunny" Cooper, whom Pincus brought up from South Africa; U.S. expert Milton Lang, under contract as Director of Production now, after some years with Near East Air Transport, Director of European Services; and Financial Adviser Herbert Cranko, a worldly Johannesburg attorney who set up Universal Air Services for the South African Zionists; Passenger Service Supervisor David Bar-Nes, a Dutch lawyer who came to Israel from a Nazi concentration camp and served as Commercial Representative for K.L.M. until he joined El Al in 1950; and hardworking technical specialist Curley Wimbourne, another South African under contract as Director of Maintenance.

El Al's ground crews have come a long way since 1949 when 75% of the 350 company employees were non-Israeli, and they have licked the maintenance problems connected with operating early-model Constellations over 12,000 miles of trunk routes. Three modernized L-049's went into service in 1951-2 and the DC-4's were sold. Hundreds of young Israelis have been trained by the foreign experts, so that 70% of all maintenance work is handled at Lydda. Only 60 of the imported technicians remain; there are also 50 foreign air crew under contract.

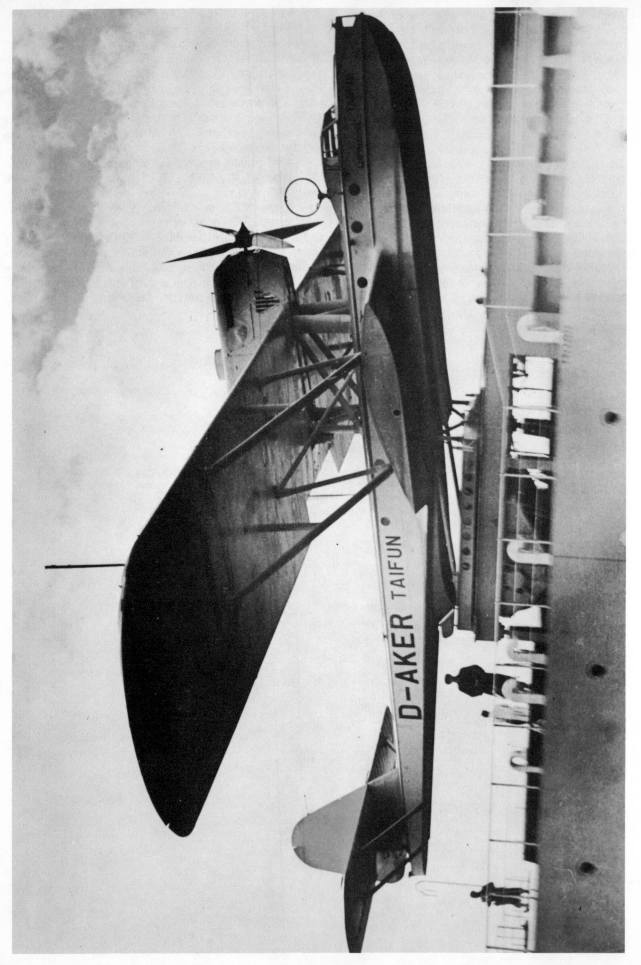

German Lufthansa carried on development of catapult-launched craft operating from trans-atlantic steamers. Here Dornier WAL is prepared for flight.

Lufthansa catapult seaplane operations were brought to a high peak of efficiency. Blohm & Voss *HA 139* was one of later types.

Small transports, such as this Koolhoven FK-43, were in demand for short hops in Europe.

Air France Breuget 530 was eighteen-passenger seaplane capable of 125 mph.

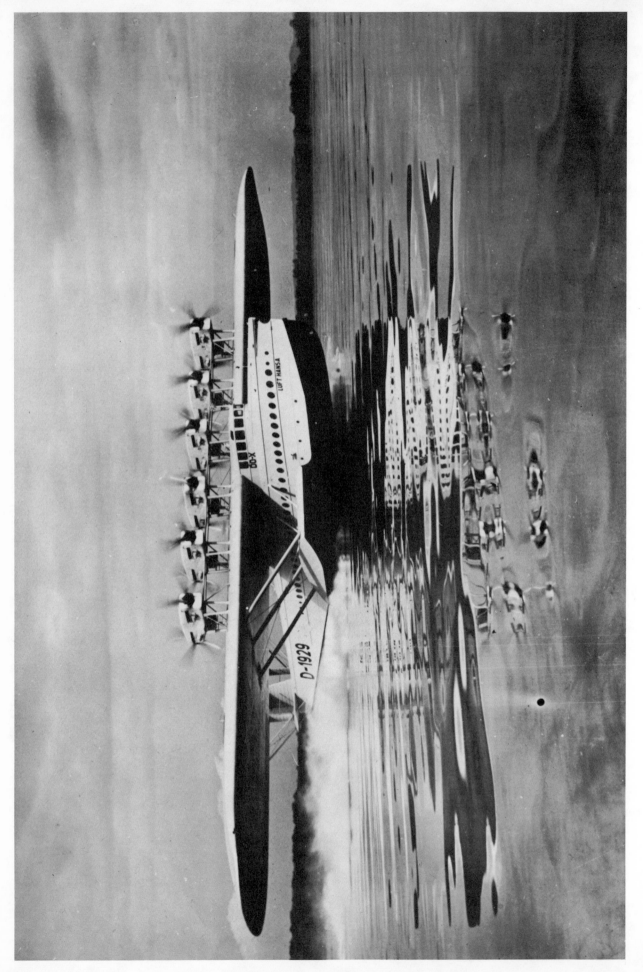

Dornier DO-X with 12 engines was sensation of early 1930's air travel with capacity of 160 passengers.

KLM-ROYAL DUTCH AIRLINE

PRESENT DAY KLM is the proof that it was indeed possible to organize it! But since the mailing of that circular and K.L.M. of today, many difficulties had to be overcome and people had to be convinced about the practicability of the aeroplane as a means of transport.

K.L.M. had its origin in the ELTA organized by the young Lieutenant Albert Plesman. Plesman was K.L.M.'s first manager. Founded in 1919 it is now the oldest airline in the World.

Flying was only started in May 1920. Two passengers, clad like North Pole travellers, flew in an open aeroplane which had been chartered. The former military flying field near the capital of the Netherlands, 13 feet below sea level, was chosen as civil airport. Before closing down the service on the 31st of October (then flying only took place in summer!), a service had also been opened to Hamburg and Copenhagen. With some considerable ceremony the services were resumed in April 1921. In the past few years several cities in Europe were included in the K.L.M. network. The first Fokker aircraft carried the passengers in closed cabins, which meant a considerable progress.

At the foundation in 1919 planes had already been under consideration to extend activities outside Europe. The company was then already named "Royal Dutch Airlines for the Netherlands aɩ.d Colonies." In 1920 the government of the East Indies and a newspaper offered large amounts of money to the pilot who flew to Java within a certain time. At that time a suitable type of aircraft for such a flight had not yet been constructed. That was the case in 1924, when a Fokker F-7, constructed of wood, linen and aluminum, completed the flight in 51 days (but including a compulsory delay of a month in Turkey). A pioneer flight across high mountains and primeval forests without radio and at times in tropical down-pours and violent gusts of wind.

The first passenger on the East Indian route was an American, Van Lear Black, who chartered an aircraft complete with crew in 1927. In more than five weeks they flew to Batavia and back. Thereafter, it went quicker. In 1930 there was a scheduled service, which became three flights a week in 1947. The East Indies was drawn ever closer to the Netherlands. Or in the words of the journalist Johan Koning in a booklet he wrote about the Hague: "The Hague — a cool suburb of Batavia situated on the North Sea Coast."

Some remarkable feats were recorded for this route — the backbone of the K.L.M. in those pre-war years. One of these was the Christmas mail flight with the Pelican in 1933 in 100 hours and the flight of the Uiver in the race, though not a scheduled flight, was a great success and resulted in a first prize in the handicap class.

In Europe the network was extended further and the latest technical improvements were introduced. Radiotelephony and telegraphy and the air-cooled engine had put in an appearance. The service to passengers was improved and airhostesses became regular members of the Flying Dutchman crews. The larger Fokker aircraft were followed by the all metal American aeroplanes and K.L.M. was the first European airline to put them into service. At the outbreak of the second World War K.L.M. operated a European network extending from Oslo in the extreme North to Naples in the South.

Once the Far Eastern service got going, the Netherlands, Antilles and Surinam were connected by air with the mother country by the flight of the Snip in 1934. The first K.L.M. flight across the Ocean had been accomplished! Next the West Indies network was planned and gradually extended. Thus K.L.M. prospered. By uniting all efforts in the Netherlands into one national airline and the tradition of the Dutch as a carrying nation, were the cause that the Netherlands — one of the smaller nations — joined the ranks of the great aviation powers.

Then the war came. Schiphol was soon in power of the aggressor. Aviation in Europe was practically at a standstill. Only the Bristol-Lisbon service, later on extended to Gibralter, was still in operation. The fact that one of the planes was shot down over the Bay of Biscay and another escaped by the skin of its teeth, goes to show the difficulties encountered. In the West flying went on during the war and the network was even extended. The Far Eastern route was kept going for quite a long time still, at first from Naples and later on from Tel Aviv. When the East Indies were occupied in 1942 the flights on this route also came to an end.

When the Netherlands were liberated in May 1945, Schiphol the home port of the Flying Dutchman was one complete ruin. There were over 200 bomb craters in platform and runways and of all the buildings only one wall remained standing. The entire technical and commercial equipment had to be reconstructed. The purchase of aircraft was of course of vital importance to K.L.M. During the war 18 aircraft had been destroyed and 8 had been damaged. It would be necessary to obtain new aircraft without delay if K.L.M. were to remain in the running as an international airline. Mr. Plesman who had been exiled to Twente in the eastern part of the Netherlands had got his plans all worked out. On the day of the liberation he had departed for America via Great Britain. He returned with 18-skymasters and later on further aircraft were purchased. These had seen duty in the war just ended. K.L.M. had to make up a great deal of leeway, especially when compared with Britain and American aviation. Reconstruction was taken in hand energetically. The first international service to be reopened was (of course) the Far Eastern Route. It was necessary to have a fast service for passengers and freight to the East Indies in connection with the situation there after the liberation. For that reason this service came first and was in operation even before any of the services in Europe were reopened. In December 1945 the first of these — the service to Copenhagen — was started again. In 1946 all pre-war services in Europe were reopened and new ones were added to the network. K.L.M. extended its network continually under the inspiring guidance of the late Fr. Dr. Plesman, who in 1947 received the

Five rode in cabin of this TWA Consolidated *Fleetster* first American all-metal monocoque fuselage transport.

honorary degree in the technical sciences from the Technical University for his achievements in the field of international aviation. Dr. Plesman directed K.L.M. for more than 34 years. He died unexpectedly in 1953 on New Year's Eve. His advice "the air ocean unites all peoples" will be found over his bust in the hall of the K.L.M. head office in the Hague.

The resumption of the traditional part of the country in world traffic was of importance for an early economic construction of the Netherlands and this was understood only too well by the government and the city of Amsterdam. Schiphol was rebuilt so far that some months after the liberation it could be used for air traffic again. The fleet consisting of 51 aircraft in 1939 comprised 75 units in 1956. A year after the liberation the network had been extended to twice its pre-war length.

Notwithstanding the fact that K.L.M. had to start from scratch it was the first European airline to inaugurate a North Atlantic service after the war. In the following years the other continents were also included in the network. This required modern aircraft. For that reason K.L.M. operated with those passenger aircraft which were most in demand all over the world. After the DC-4 and the Skymaster the DC-6, DC-6B, the Constellation and the Super-Constellation were put into service. The DC-3 was replaced on the European stretches by the comfortable and fast Convair, which in its turn will be replaced by the Viscount, the first aircraft with turbo-prop engines to be put into service by K.L.M. The DC-7C "Seven-Seas" will be the last piston engined aircraft operated on the long hauls, until the jet passenger aircraft DC-8 will take its place in 1960. There is still another new type of turbo-prop aircraft, the Lockheed Electra, on order by K.L.M. which among other routes will be used on services to the Middle East. The fleet of aircraft now consisting of 86 planes will be extended in 1957 with the arrival ot 9 Vickers Viscounts and 10 DC-7C's. Such a huge fleet of aircraft has to be backed by an up-to-date and extensive technical operational, commercial and administrative organization. At present, some 8,700 K.L.M. employees are at work at Schipol, the home base of K.L.M. In all, the company employs well over 16,000

persons. A powerful, international airline has been built in ten years' time which can in no way be compared with the pre-war company. K.L.M. now serves 118 cities in 74 countries, whereas these figures were 61 and 29 in 1939.

K.L.M. not only carries passengers, though they number 2,250 daily or since the liberation 5,800,000 passengers, but freight and mail as well. Freight traffic has developed even faster than passenger traffic. In 1956 nearly 24,000,000 kg. freight were carried by K.L.M. In 1920 it amounted to 22,000 kg. Special freight planes are used and to New York alone there are three services a week and during a part of the winter even six. The primitive office of the Schipol station master, used in pre-war days as a storage room, has made way for a large up-to-date freight building, in which an animal hotel is also housed. Live animal transport has in part become a specialty of K.L.M. Elephants (accompanied by the traditional Dutch hen which quietens the animals during the flight) and horses (according to the experts of the University of Utrecht the aircraft is the best means of transport for these animals) constitute a large part of this traffic.

In October 1953 the first prize was won with one of the freighters, which has been specially converted for passengers traffic, in the handicap class of the Christ church race.

The results of K.L.M. from a financial point of view are satisfactory as well, though large amounts have to be invested. An amount of F.fl. 200 million is involved in the purchase of the eight DC-8 aircraft. The introduction of the tourist class especially across the Atlantic has influenced the increase of the turnover. A profit was made in the post-war years with the exception of 1949, so that since 1953 the shareholders could regularly be paid a dividend.

K.L.M. has also made a name in the field of aerial survey. Large territories (i.e. in Austria, Syria and Surinam) have been mapped by its aerial survey department.

Thus K.L.M. has grown into a vigorous paying concern, ranking foremost among the great outlines of the world and placing the Netherlands in aviation immediately after the United States.

United Airlines pilots were left out in the cold when at the controls of the Boeing *Monomail*.

KLM operated the Koolhoven FK-48 twin engined six-passenger model within Holland & Denmark.

Swissair chose the De Havilland Rapid (DH 89) for short run use.

Four motor DeHavilland *DH 86* had a capacity of twelve, cruised at 173 mph.

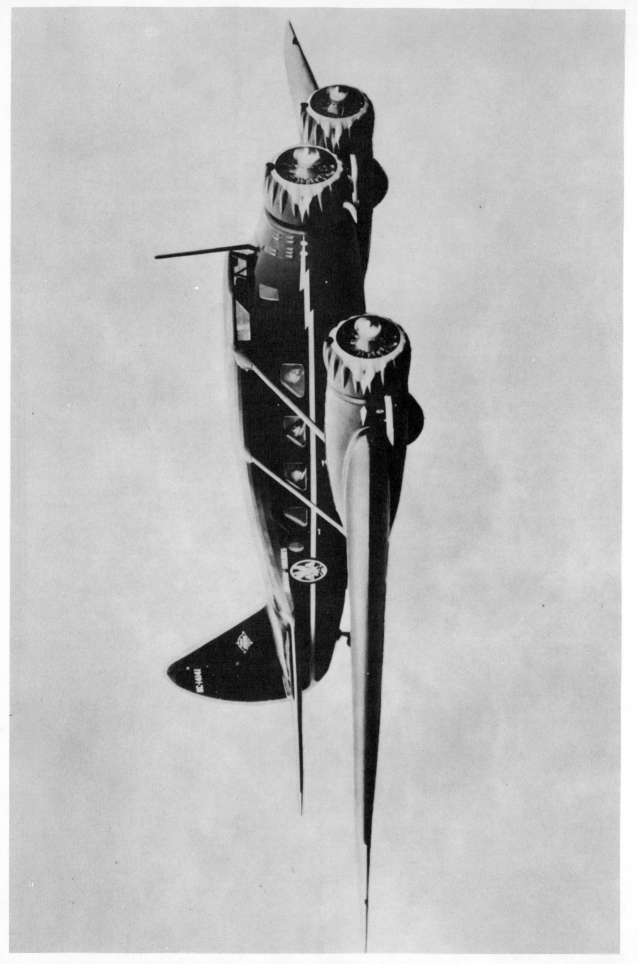

Stinson *Trimotor* was extremely modern when introduced in 1931. Carried eight passengers at 160 mph.

LUFTHANSA-GERMAN AIRLINES

GERMANY occupies a prominent place in the history of world aviation. The country has been a consistent leader in aeronautical research and in the application of the latest developments to its pioneer projects. The nation's early exploration and later setting up of long distance transocean and transcontinental air route has firmly identified Germany with the beginnings and ultimate emergence of this particular transportation medium.

Lufthansa German Airlines played an important role in establishing this heritage for Germany, the company and its predecessor being instrumental in opening up air routes within Europe and South America, between Europe and Asia, and across the North and South Atlantic. Germany as early as 1917 started air mail service between Duenaberg and the Crimea, and in 1918 followed this with an air mail route between Berlin, Hanover and Cologne.

These post-war years, however, were marked by unstable and inadequate communications within Germany, the railroads operating under severe limitations and beset by strikes. At the time, the primary means of passenger and postal transport were the railroads, and their problems were such that the General Post Office, seeking reliable and efficient delivery service for mail, documents and newspapers, brought its case before a nationwide convention at Weimar, then the seat of the National Assembly.

As an outcome of demands made at the convention by the General Post Office and others, **Deutsche Luftreederei,** a German commercial airline was organized in 1918 and the following year, in January 1919, was licensed by the German Government. On February 5, Deutsche Luftreederie inaugurated regular air service along the Berlin — Leipzig — Weimar route, reducing time for the delivery of mail from five days to four hours. Later the same year the Berlin-Hamburg route was added, and another service from Berlin via Hamburg to the Rhine and Ruhr industrial area.

By the end of 1919, Deutsche Luftreederie's airmail network within Germany's borders had grown to the point where route extensions to other European countries were the obvious next step. To enable Germany's commercial aircraft to fly along the airways of other European countries, the Deutsche Luftreederei entered into negotiations with the newly formed Dutch (KLM) and Danish carriers. An air route Copenhagen — Hamburg — Amsterdam resulted from these meetings and was operated on a pool basis, meaning that the service was maintained jointly by the companies of all three countries. The route was operated successfully until a shortage of high-grade aviation fuel forced a temporary suspension.

While the operation between Germany, Denmark, and Holland was being set up, negotiations were also underway to establish an association of European air carriers. Later the same year, this organization was set up under the name of the Association of European Operators, and later, much on initiative from Berlin, became the International Air Traffic Association, or IATA.

The name of the organization was changed in 1945 to the International Air Transport Association. The primary condition of membership in the early days was the operation of an international air service according to an official published time table.

In 1920, Deutsche Luftreederei aircraft logged 375,000 kilometers — almost 200,000 miles — using 19 German airports. The air agreement of 1921 with Lithuania, Latvia and Finland extended service on a new route from Berlin to Riga, via Stettin, Koeslin, Stolp, Danzig, Koenigsberg, and Memel, and in 1922 the first German commercial aircraft flew to England. This led to a further pool agreement with an English company, whereby a route and scheduled service were set up between London and Amsterdam, Bremen, Hamburg, and Berlin. Meanwhile the **Junkers Airline,** a German carrier established by the famous German aircraft manufacturer, inaugurated service from Budapest to Vienna, Munich, Zurich, and Geneva. Night flights, previously untried, were started in 1924 between Berlin and Stockholm, and from Berlin to Strettin and Copenhagen.

The initial success of the Luftreederei and the fact that the German Government was prepared to back financially the development of commercial aviation, led to the formation of many German airlines during this period. Also, the German Government was very successful in its international negotiations, making agreements with other European governments. By 1923, there were over 30 companies engaged in a competitive struggle, duplicating air service throughout Germany and the rest of Europe, preventing profitable operation by any one company. A need for consolidation was clearly indicated, and consequently, in 1923, the many separate operations were molded into two airlines, the **Deutsche Aero-Lloyd** and the **Junkers Luftverkehr.** The Deutsche Aero-Lloyd was formed through the joint efforts and support of the Deutsche Bank and the steamship lines, North German Lloyd and Hamburg-America, all guided by the German Government. Incidentally, the Junkers Aircraft Works, the parent organization of which the Junkers Airline was a division, developed the F-13, the world's first all-metal commercial aircraft. The F-13 was a predecessor of the three-engine Junker JU-52 which in a few years was to form the backbone of the Lufthansa fleet, and which also was the model for the equally famous American plane, the Ford-Trimotor. Both the JU-52 and the Ford Trimotor were extensively used by pioneering airlines on both sides of the Atlantic, and played a major role in blazing the long-distance aviation trails used by airlines today.

Soon even the German Aero-Lloyd and Junkers Airlines ran into difficulties. Both depended substantially on government funds, and the mushrooming growth of both again created a competitive situation which began to destroy the strength of each, and put an unnecessary double strain on the German economy. The growing air networks of other countries throughout Europe further drained what was then at best a limited

Junkers JU-52 was Lufthansa standby. Cruising speed was 152 mph.

market. Consequently, the German Air Communications Ministry, a government agency, brought pressure to bear for consolidation of Aero-Lloyd and the Junker Airline into a single organization.

The result was **Deutsche Lufthansa Aktiengesellschaft,** created January 6, 1926, as a joint private and government enterprise. Management, despite government subsidy, was totally in the hands of private interests, a condition which remains today. 36% of the new company's capital stock was held by the German government, 19% by the German provincial governments, 27.5% by the two former airlines, and 17.5% by private interests. The capital of the company was increased to 25 millions RM (Reichsmark) and Lufthansa was henceforth recognized as Germany's chosen instrument for the development of commercial aviation. Its goals and purpose of being were defined as follows, these principles applying as much today as they did 30 years ago:

(1) To link Germany with the European centers of commerce and industry, and to do so on a reciprocal basis with major foreign airline companies.

(2) To bring German cities into the existing European air networks of other countries.

(3) To provide Germany with air connections to those countries outside Europe with which close trade ties existed. These were mainly countries in North and South America and the Far East.

Though Lufthansa operated flights that first winter on a non-schedule, weather-permitting basis, its first day of scheduled operation was April 6, 1926. It flew a total of 3.8 million miles that year with a fleet of 120 aircraft, 41 of which were multi-engine and classified as long-range aircraft.

Lufthansa immediately embarked on a long series of technical advances and pioneering moves toward building the airline and the industry as a whole to what it is today. Leaders of the airline early dedicated themselves to the dual objectives of making commercial aviation both profitable and safe to the extreme. That first year, the airline was already exploring the possibility of flying at night and under inclement weather conditions, conditions which up till then considerably hindered any sort of scheduled operation. Unable to contend with these conditions, all scheduled flights were limited to the clear daylight hours, and routes of more than one day's flight time had to be terminated at nightfall, and begun again the next morning. In 1926, Lufthansa erected a series of beacons along its air routes, and flew the first combined mail and passenger night flights on the scheduled runs between Berlin and Koenigsberg. This service connected in Koenigsberg with flights to Moscow operated by Deruluft the Russo-German airline, thereby making one-day service possible between Berlin and Moscow.

The airline at this point in its development operated a maintenance and overhaul base in Staaken, near Berlin, and shortly thereafter opened a second one at Stuttgart. The airline in 1926 made a big advance in airline safety and set an aviation precedent by constructing a chain of 13 radio stations along its routes as navigational aids.

Long-distance exploration also got underway this first year with proving flights to the Far East, using the G-24, an early three-engine aircraft built by the Junkers Company. On July 23, 1926, three of the aircraft took off from Berlin to Peking on what was to be a five-week odyssey across Russia and China. The flight time, though a small life time by pilots' standards today, was considered extraordinary for those days. That same year a Dornier Wal flying boat was sent to Brazil by ship to explore routes within the South American continent and the possibility of eventual transocean flights across the Atlantic.

Lufthansa made the first flight across the Alps from Munich to Milan on April 13, 1927, in preparation for a service from Munich to Rome. Also that year, a route was extended from Berlin to Oslo via Copenhagen and Goeteborg. The airline in 1928 began night flights between Paris and London, and the travel time between Berlin and Leningrad had been reduced from the 70-hour rail time to 14 air hours. By 1929, the routes across the Alps to Italy and across the Baltic Sea to Scandinavia were firmly established. Joint air/rail services had been introduced, and the Lufthansa network stood at roughly 25,000 miles.

Though these first years of the new young industry were ones marked by frequent milestones, though brave adventures and pioneers repeatedly gained prestige for themselves and their countries, Lufthansa's bold advances during these years were primarily inspired by a determination to make commercial aviation a business success. Whatever history the airline made during these years was incidental to a well-planned program of development.

Lufthansa's main aim from the outset was to establish and make practical long-range, intercontinental air routes. With an operational network covering most of Europe, the stage was set for a major attempt to bridge the Atlantic Ocean. In 1925, an affiliate of Lufthansa called the Condor Syndicate, had been formed in Columbia to study the possibility of an air service between South America and Europe, and had established a base on the Island of Fernando Noronha, just off the coast of Brazil. The Dornier Wal flying boat, sent to South America in 1926, flew experimental flights throughout that continent making a study of the feasibility of transatlantic flying and an operation within that continent. In the course of these experiments, the Wal flew non-stop from Rio de Janeiro to Buenos Aires. The Condor Syndicate in 1927 obtained Brazilian traffic rights and opened routes from Porto Alegre to Rio de Janeiro and Natal. As the Condor Syndicate was laying the groundwork in South America, a similar step-by-step extension of the European network was taking place to bring routes down the African coast to a point where the transocean distance between Africa and South America would be cut to a minimum.

With an eye to extending its network south, Lufthansa concluded an agreement with Iberia, the Spanish airline organized with Lufthansa's financial cooperation, whereby the German carrier was allowed to use the route Berlin — Barcelona, later Berlin — Madrid. In 1927 a Junker F-13, fitted with pontoons, was put on the North German Lloyd steamer "Lutzow", in order to carry out

Air France employed Junkers *JU-52* models on long runs, carrying seventeen passengers.

a series of landing and catapult launching tests en route to the Canary Islands. A year later, a Dornier Wal flying boat made the trip alone to the Canary Islands, thus paving the way for a flight in 1929 from Berlin to Las Palmas, via Seville and Tenerife. That same year, as a result of a decision by the German Post Office to institute flights exclusively for mail instead of having it carried on scheduled passenger aircraft, the first direct postal service was flown between Berlin and Seville, covering the distance in 15 hours.

To cut down mail delivery time between continents, which was the main objective, a relay system was adapted for South Atlantic crossings, using the services of Lufthansa and the Condor Syndicate for the land portions, steamship lines for the transatlantic portion of the trip. The mail caught up to the steamer at its last port of call on one side of the ocean, and was met by a flying boat at its first port of call on the other side. On March 22, 1930, a Dornier Wal flying boat of the Condor Syndicate, taking off from Rio de Janeiro, caught up with a Hamburg-bound steamer at the island of Fernando Noronha, cutting two days from the usual transit time for mail. If sent by steamer all the way, mail took as long as 13 to 15 days. On April 18, in the opposite direction, a flying boat met the steamer in Bahia, Brazil, and flew ahead with the mail to Rio de Janeiro, thus again cutting two days from the old time. Starting in July 1930, this was made a regular service, the mail flown from Germany to the island of Las Palmas, put aboard a ship which took it to Fernando Noronha, where it was met by a Condor Syndicate aircraft and flown to Rio de Janeiro.

This operation could cut as much as ten days from the round trip time to a get a letter and reply between Berlin and Rio de Janeiro. Fourteen such flights each way took place that first year. This operation was considerably improved when, later in 1930, a joint service was established between Lufthansa, the Condor Syndicate, and Germany's Zeppelins, the latter operating in addition to steamers across the South Atlantic. The route used was Berlin-Seville-Recife-Buenos Aires, a distance of roughly 8000 miles which by the new combination was covered in six days, taking only five days to Rio.

Test flights were continually underway, throughout 1931 and 1932, pushing farther down the African coast, diminishing the eventual transatlantic distance to be crossed. A number of proving flights were operated during 1930 on a route from Germany to England, then down to La Coruna and Cadiz in Spain, Las Palmas and finally Villa Cisneros, a city in Spanish West Africa. In 1931, two flights were flown south as far as Bathurst, British Gambia, the closest point in Africa to the South American coast. The combined flight and zeppelin time between Berlin and Rio de Janeiro in 1932 was reduced to four days, eight days Berlin-Santiago. Also that year the Dornier X, an enormous-for-its-day flying boat with twelve engines, was first used in South America.

Still to be overcome, however, was the problem of flying limited-range aircraft over approximately 2000 miles of ocean. No planes then had the fuel capacity to make the trip. It was at this time, in 1932, that Lufthansa put into effect an idea it had long considered and been working towards: motherships for its fleet of flying boats. That year the airline leased the steamer "Westfalen: and converted it to a fully-equipped floating air base for the flying boats. The problem of landing the aircraft and getting them on the ship was solved by a drift sail — a floating dock made of heavy but pliable material — which served as a mooring place for the aircraft after it had landed. The flying boat could then be lifted aboard the ship with a crane, and, after being fueled and servied, launched again by means of Heinkel steam or compressed-air catapults. The first experimental flight was made in 1933, by a Dornier Wal between Bathurst and Natal, refuelling on the "Westfalen", which was stationed approximately midway on the aircraft's route. The new time between Bathurst and Natal — 15 hours. This historic first scheduled flight took place on February 3, 1934, with the relay handled as follows:

Stuttgart	to Seville	—Heinkel
Seville	to Bathurst (2000 miles)	—Junkers JU-52
Bathurst	to Natal	—Dornier Wal flying boat
Natal	to Buenos Aires	—an aircraft of the Condor Syndicate

Lapsed time for the 8000 mile journey was slightly less than four days. Original fortnightly schedule was soon doubled to weekly service, and Lufthansa operated 24 round trip flights during 1934.

The next five years were marked by extension of Lufthansa's network and facilities on the South Atlantic route. New aircraft were introduced, such as the diesel-powered Dornier DC-18, and still a larger model flying boat, the "10-ton-Wal", an improved version of the original Wal. The Blohm and Voss Ha-138, a four-engine, advanced design seaplane, soon took over the chores of the Dornier Wal on the transatlantic flights. Lufthansa purchased two more ships, the "Schwabenland" in 1934, and the "Ostmark" in 1936, converting them also to floating bases for the flying boats. One ship was stationed off Spanish West Africa, the other off Brazil. By 1935 the flight time between Berlin and Rio de Janeiro was down to 3½ days, only three days between Berlin and Buenos Aires. That fall the mail service was extended to Santiago, a trip then taking six days. Frankfurt in 1936 replaced Stuttgart as the base in Germany for the transatlantic operation, and the Natal-Rio de Janeiro sector of the Condor Syndicate's network was taken over by Lufthansa. By 1939, when service on this route was suspended due to the war, Lufthansa had made over 500 scheduled flights between Germany and South America.

Lufthansa by no means centered all its activities during these years on the South Atlantic. Parallel efforts were being made to improve mail service between North America and Europe. The airline first provided a joint air/sea mail service across the North Atlantic in 1928, connecting with the mail boat "Columbia" in Bremerhaven and flying on to Berlin, Frankfurt, and Munich. The first catapult flights took place the following year from the ocean liner "Bremen", which was specially adapted to carry a small Heinkel seaplane. The first

Somewhat like Junkers trimotor was this Dewoitine *338* in Air France service before WWII. Seating capacity was eighteen, 173 mph cruising.

flight from the "Bremen" was on June 22, 1929, when the seaplane was launched about 280 miles off New York, a trip which, only 2½ hours by air, shortened the mail run between Germany and the United States by 24 hours. On the return trip to Europe of the "Bremen" on August 1, the Heinkel was catapulted from the ship at a point five miles west of Cherbourg for the 550-mile, four-hour flight to Bremerhaven, where another plane flew the mail the rest of the way to Berlin's Tempelhof Airport. This trip cut 36 hours from the New York-Berlin mail run. The third such operation August 15th was undertaken with two planes, one catching up to the westbound steamer while it was at Cherbourg, its last port of call in Europe, another catapulted from the ship as it approached New York. Time saved: Two days.

In 1930, the "Europa" was also fitted with catapult gear, and further equipment and procedural modifications increased the range of the operation to 750 miles. For the next five years, until late in 1935, gradual improvements were made until the range of the catapult service was increased to 1250 miles and the trip between New York and Berlin was a matter of 4½ days. Almost 200 catapult flights were completed by late that year. The mother ship "Schwabenland" was moved into the North Atlantic in 1936, preparatory to trial runs of the two Dornier DO-18 flying boats on a southerly route from Lisbon to New York via the Azores and Bermuda. Four round trip crossings took place that year, the "Schwabenland" shuttling back and forth between New York and the Azores to service both the east-and-westbound flights. The following year fourteen crossings were made, four of them with the new larger and more powerful Blohm and Voss Ha-139, and an additional catapult ship, the "Friesenland", was put into service on the North Atlantic. By later that year Lufthansa was ready to begin regular scheduled services over this route, and in 1938 operated 26 flights successfully and without incident.

The third direction of Lufthansa's early exploration and expansion, after firmly establishing its domestic and intra-European routes, was to the East. Though in this direction no oceans barred the way, a number of technical and political obstacles did exist. A direct route from Berlin to Tokyo, for instance, passed over 5540 miles of country only sparsely inhabited, much of it uncharted, with few if any facilities for aircraft, and any alternate route was considerably longer (present Lufthansa southern Frankfurt-Tokyo route over 9000 miles). The heroic early attempts to establish this link are a fine example of the pioneer spirit so much a part of the aviation industry of that time. As was the case in the development of service across the North and South Atlantic, Lufthansa proceeded step by step, working gradually toward the eventual setting up of a route spanning all of Asia.

Operation of a route to the Far East via Russia was the first stage of the plan. On July 23, 1926, Lufthansa dispatched two Junkers G-24's to explore an air route to Peiping (Peking) via Moscow. This expedition reached its destination successfully seven days and over 6000 miles later, making the return flight to Berlin's Tempelhof Airport the following December. Two years later a Lufthansa Junkers W-33 made two reconnaissance

flights to Irkutsk, in southern Siberia, the second flight, covering a route of 7500 miles, completed in a little over 76 hours.

The first leg of the southern route to the Far East was explored in 1929, when an Arado V-1 mail plane was flown round trip Berlin-Istanbul between October 25 and 29, 1929. This route was extended on November 10, 1930, as far as Baghdad. Later that year, in April, scheduled airmail service was inaugurated on a route from Vienna to Istanbul, via Budapest, Belgrade and Sofia, an extension which formally brought Lufthansa's network to the borders of Asia Minor. Though Lufthansa during this time carried on negotiations with the Russo-German carrier, Deruluft, to establish a route between the Far East and Europe, its first real advance in this sphere of operation was the formation on February 21, 1930, of the Chino-German airline **Eurasia,** owned jointly by the Chinese Transport Ministry (two-thirds) and Lufthansa (one-third). Incidentally, Lufthansa's one-third share in the airline was a contribution of aircraft, technical equipment and personnel, while the bulk of the financial burden fell to the Chinese government. Eurasia was subsequently responsible for building up air service in the Far East, particularly within China.

From this point on, many of the pioneering flights undertaken by Lufthansa were done in connection with the delivery of aircraft to Eurasia, its new Far East holding. While some of the aircraft were shipped out by rail, others were flown out by adventurous Lufthansa pilots, such as the three men who ferried three Junkers W-34's from Germany to China in 1933 via Siberia. In 1934, a three-engine JU-52, piloted by von Gablenz, President of Lufthansa and father of one of Lufthansa's present flight captains, made the first successful flight from Berlin to Shanghai. Von Gablenz followed a course via Cairo, Baghdad, Djask, Calcutta, Bangkok and Canton, and made the trip in 69 hours. This historic flight via the southern route to the Far East supplied a wealth of data on weather and flight conditions necessary for any kind of scheduled operation to follow. The second stage of Lufthansa's Far East plan materialized in 1937, when a mail route was opened between Berlin and Baghdad.

Exploration of a route to China by way of Kabul, Afghanistan's capital, the Pamir Mountains and East Turkestan — about 1200 miles shorter than the southern route via India — was accomplished with a test flight in 1936. The Junkers Airline in 1924 had started a service in Persia (Iran), called **Luftverkehr Persien.** This airline operated Junkers F-13's out of Teheran, flying to the Russian border, connecting there with the Russian air network; it also flew between Teheran and Bushire, a seaport on the Persian Gulf. Lufthansa extended its network to Teheran in April 1938, and several months later pushed this route on to Kabul, via Herat. This route, running Berlin, Vienna, Athens, Isle of Rhodes, Damascus, Baghdad, Teheran was originally for mail only, but was later expanded to include passengers.

The longest flight yet undertaken in the Far East — the trip from Berlin to Tokyo on the southern route via Basra (Iraq), Karachi, and Hanoi — was started No-

Sleek Fokker F-20 was ultimate development of high-wing trimotor. KLM flew these twenty-passenger models.

vember 28, 1938, as a demonstration run by Lufthansa of the new four-engine Focke Wulf FW 200 "Condor", one of the first aircraft to have retractable landing gear, and capable of speeds upward of 200 miles per hour. Also, Lufthansa wanted to get information on airports and ground facilities in Japan, and to have conferences with the Japanese national airline prior to establishing scheduled air service between Germany and Japan. The 8500-mile trip was completed in the record time of 42 hours, and was flown by the same crew which previously set a speed record Berlin-New York-Berlin. This and subsequent proving flights led to inauguration in July, 1939, of scheduled service Berlin-Bangkok, a 6250-mile route taking 4½ days via Vienna, Athens, Beirut, Baghdad, Basra, Djask, Karachi, Jodphur, Alabad, Calcutta and Rangoon.

In September, 1939, when service was terminated to all but the neutral countries, the Lufthansa network embraced all of Europe, and reached across the Atlantic to both North and South America. The airline had an extensive subsidiary operation both in South America and the Far East, besides operating its own Middle and Far East routes, with every indication of an agreement with the Japanese national carrier within a matter of months. Its last full year of operation showed 177,000 passengers carried, over 11,000,000 miles flown, 52,619 flight movements within Germany, and 13,483 in other countries.

During the war years, service was continued within Germany as well as on routes to Turkey, Italy, Spain and Portugal. In April, 1945, all service was suspended. Lufthansa's subsidiary, Eurasia, became China Air Transportation Corporation, the Chinese National Government airline. Lufthansa was not officially liquidated until January 1, 1951.

Germany since the war had been subject to occupation laws, control of air sovereignty in West Germany exercised by three High Commissioners. Though the country was forging ahead in a full-scale industrial recovery, aviation was at a standstill because of a ban on any kind of flying. Transport Minister Seebohm repeatedly drew attention to the need for a German air service, and only gradually was the right to use the German airports transferred to the federal and state governments. Though the Federal Republic became a sovereign state in October, 1954, full air sovereignty was not restored to West Germany until May, 1955, at which time West Germany regained its right to engage in aviation activities, such as the development of an air transport industry, and manufacture of aircraft.

Long before the restoration of air sovereignty, however, forces were at work to revive interest in Germany's once-flourishing aviation industry. Just two months after Lufthansa's official liquidation in 1951, Hans M. Bongers, the airline's former traffic manager, was appointed advisor in aviation matters to Dr. Hans C. Seebohm, West Germany's Minister of Transport. The Bongers Bureau, as it came to be known, had its headquarters in Cologne.

In 1952, the Minister of Transport set up a parliamentary committee to study the practicality of eventually organizing a German national airline. Dr. Kurt Weigelt, Lufthansa's former Chairman of the Board of Control, headed the new group. In November of that year, after thorough analysis, Weigelt's committee submitted its report to the Minister of Transport, affirming the advisibility of a German airline. On the basis of this, and with the approval of the Allied Powers, the Federal Cabinet agreed to the formation of a preliminary company. The Federal Transport Ministry, with the participation of the German Federal Railroad and the state of Nordrhein-Westfalen, created a share-holding company for aviation on January 6, 1953, called **Aktiengesellschaft fuer Luftverkehr, or Luftag,** with head offices in Cologne. Dr. Weigelt was appointed Chairman, with Hans M. Bongers and Gerhard Hoeltje as members of the Board. Original capital was set at six million Deutsche Mark (DM), but was soon increased to 25 million DM to allow for purchase of aircraft and setting up a crew training program.

At the outset, Luftag, was faced with three major problems: 1) Choice of aircraft; 2) selection of an operations, maintenance and overhaul base; 3) organizing a training program.

Influencing the company's decision on aircraft was the fact that the airline was coming into existence at a time when the industry was on the threshold of the Jet Age, when jet aircraft were an aspect of the very near future. It had to assess the merits of various short-range and long-range piston aircraft already proven by their airlines, yet have an eye to the day not far off when the same aircraft would either have to measure up to competition from jets, or be sold, or converted to some other use. With all points considered, Lufthansa's first order in 1953 was for four Lockheed 1049-G Super Constellations for the proposed intercontinental routes, and four two-engine Convair CV-340's for the European flights. Three Douglas DC-3's were purchased a short time later as all-purpose aircraft to fill gaps in the proposed schedule, and four more Super Constellations were ordered in 1955.

As for the second problem, all indications at the time were that Hamburg would be the center of operations. Most of the proposed flights were planned to originate and terminate at that city's Fuhlsbuettel Airport, making it the most logical place for a maintenance and overhaul base. The real nerve center of a modern airline is its aircraft ground facility, and an estimated 25% to 30% of an airline's total personnel are employed in this branch of the business. Considering this, Lufthansa began construction in Hamburg on what was to be Europe's largest and most advanced installation of this kind. It was started as a single large hangar and machine shop, was later expanded with the addition of another hangar of similar proportions, a test stand for engines, and a number of other specialized structures. Construction on the base was begun long before the actual introduction of scheduled flights.

The matter of training presented probably the most serious problem. For one thing, and most important, any pilot training program had to be started from scratch. Due to the ten-year cessation of all aviation activity within Germany, there was not as there was elsewhere a ready supply of pilots trained to any level of flight proficiency, or abreast of the tremendous advances in aircraft, equipment and procedures intro-

Trimotor type bit the dust with DeHavilland *DH A-3*, shown here in QANTAS markings.

duced during this inactive period. In other countries a situation existed whereby military pilots could make an easy and natural transition into the ranks of civil aviation.

Further, it was essential that the airline require all applicants to speak English fluently, or make provisions in the training program to teach English, as this was more or less the adopted language of civil aviation, used predominantly in airport and radio procedures, technical manuals, IATA and CAB instructions, etc.

Meticulous attention was devoted to the selection and training of all personnel, but this applied especially to the pilots. Former captains of the old Lufthansa were interviewed and examined, but only a small percentage of these were found suitable for reemployment. Better prospects were available from among those pilots of the former German Air Force (Luftwaffe), with experience in large multi-engine aircraft. To adequately cover the airline's original planned operation, it was estimated that 70 pilots and 36 flight engineers should be selected and trained.

A flight training school with a faculty of ten experienced lecturers was opened at the Bremen airport in September, 1953, specifically for the purposes of the future airline. The school was complete with a Link trainer for instruction in instrument flying, and put the future flight crews through a rugged curriculum of such subjects as navigation, meteorology, and communications. Actual flight training at the start was conducted in Hamble, England, at the ASTC Flying School. Those destined to be crews for the Super Constellations went on to the Lockheed Aircraft Corporation training facility at Burbank, California, and those who would fly the Convairs went to the Convair Factory in San Diego, Calif. for instruction. The training in the United States concluded with their being tested for and granted commercial air pilot certificates. Flight engineers were examined for their operating certificates by the Federal Post Office in West Germany.

The flight school in Bremen was the only facility of its kind operated by a commercial airline. With the later addition of training aircraft (nine De Havilland Chipmunk 22's, two twin Beech Bonanzas, three Saab 91-B's), actual flight training was also conducted at the school. Since then, as the number of flight crews has been built up by Lufthansa to the point where no more are needed presently, the flight school has been turned over to the German Air Force for basic training of the nation's young military pilots. The school had turned out for Lufthansa by the end of 1959, 174 pilots, navigators, engineers and radio operators, with plans to turn out a total of 190 new pilots by mid-1961. The ground staff — the specialists evolving from the complex airline operation of today as compared to 30 years ago — received instruction in Germany and at the ground facilities of other airlines. Mechanics were also given an intensive six-month course in Germany in the practice and theory of aircraft maintenance and overhaul.

During its first years of operation, it was necessary for Lufthansa to borrow captains, first officers and navigators from other airlines. In an unusual gesture of interline cooperation, British European Airways (BEA) offered experienced pilots who were taken into the European Services, and pilots on loan from Trans World Airlines (TWA) and Eastern Airlines flew the long distance Super-G Constellation flights. In this way, the borrowed pilots acted as flight captains, and the new Lufthansa pilots gained practical on-the-job experience acting as co-pilots.

On August 6, 1954, The Board of Management voted to change the name of **Luftag** from **Aktiengesellschaft fuer Luftverkehrsbedarf** to **Deutsche Lufthansa Aktiengesellschaft,** and the company's capital was increased to 50 million DM. In October, the capital was increased again to 80 million DM, and in December, 1956, to 120 million DM.

During the spring of 1955 Lufthansa received permission from the Allied authorities and from the Federal Minister of Transport to begin proving flights within Germany prior to inaugurating commercial service between German airports in April, 1955. With the return of full air sovereignty to the Federal Republic in May, 1955, the last restrictions on German air transport were removed. Service to countries in Europe started on May 15, 1955, and to the United States on June 8.

Lufthansa's growth since resuming operations in 1955 has been a close parallel to West Germany's rapid economic and industrial recovery over the same period. By the time air sovereignty was returned and the company could actively conduct the operation of a commercial airline, it had already carefully and meticulously laid the plans for picking up the threads of the old network pioneered in the years between 1926 and 1939. After reestablishing the major domestic routes radiating from the two main terminals of Hamburg and Frankfurt, the airline went on later in 1955 to add the German cities of Bremen, Nuremberg, Hanover and Stuttgart. Lufthansa was not then, nor is it now, allowed to service West Berlin, by reason of a residual stipulation of the 1945 Four Power Treaty. Lisbon was included in the extraterritorial schedule for the fall of 1955, service having been resumed in May to London, Paris and Madrid. These routes were flown with the Convair 340's, the North Atlantic flights New York-Hamburg via Shannon and Dusseldorf with Super Constellations.

That first year, Lufthansa resumed service over a 13,500 mile network in Europe and to North America.

Lufthansa flew the 100,000th passenger in 1956 before its first anniversary, later that year started a twice-weekly service via Paris to New York, and another twice-weekly service from Frankfurt to Chicago via Shannon and Montreal. That August it started flying over the South Atlantic route to its old points in South America, and a month later revived the Middle East service. These route extensions to Rio de Janeiro and Buenos Aires, and to Istanbul, Beirut, Baghdad, and Teheran, were largely the result of deliveries on additional Super Constellations. The airline in 1957 received the first of four much-improved 1649-A Super Star Constellations ordered earlier that year in addition to the original orders of eight 1049-G models. Seven Vickers Armstrong 814-D Viscounts were due for delivery during 1958, and training aircraft were being

Next logical move for Fokker was from three engines to four; F22 resulted. Thirty could ride at cruising speed of 125 in this model.

added to the fleet at the Bremen Flight School.

The further addition in January, 1957, of five Convair 440 "Metropolitans" and two chartered Vickers Viscounts enabled Lufthansa in April to step up the frequency of its domestic and European flights, and expand the network to include routes Frankfurt-Stuttgart-Zurich, and Dusseldorf-Frankfurt-Munich-Vienna. Later that year, in October, another route Munich-Hanover-Hamburg-Copenhagen was inaugurated. A new run from Hamburg to Paris was started to four weekly on the Hamburg-Madrid service via Cologne and Frankfurt.

That April, Montevideo, the capital of Uruguay, was added to the Germany-South America run. The South Atlantic service had started out strictly as a first class operation, but in March, 1957, was expanded to include Tourist Class accommodations.

Lufthansa made two moves in December, 1957, that were destined to strongly influence the future growth of the airline. First, the airline's share of the North Atlantic cargo market had developed to the point where it was practical to begin an all-cargo operation. Inaugurating this service was a chartered DC-4 flying from Boston to Brussels. The cargo: a shipment of live lobsters. Second, the airline that December placed its initial order for four Boeing 707-430 Intercontinental Jets.

In 1958, non-stop Super Constellation service was inaugurated in February between New York and Frankfurt. April that year Economy fares were first offered by Lufthansa on the North Atlantic route, and Rome was added to the European network. In May, flights on the South Atlantic route were extended beyond Buenos Aires to Santiago de Chile. Two special milestones were set that summer: Lufthansa's one millionth passenger since the airline's 1955 reactivation was flown July 1; and in August, its 100,000th North Atlantic passenger since 1955 was singled out.

Delivery of the nine Vickers Viscounts ordered in 1957 started in December, 1958, at which time they were integrated into the longer segments of the European network and on runs to the Near East. November marked the inclusion of Cairo in the Near/Middle East network, and the introduction of Lufthansa's Senator Service between the United States and Germany. The Senator, a special flight, operating twice weekly each way, was something truly unique in the annals of aviation. The degree of luxury was such that there were only 32 seats on a Super Star Constellation capable ordinarily of carrying upwards of 90 people. In order to break even financially on the flight, Lufthansa had to have at least 30 passengers on board, so that it was understood from the start by the public and the airline alike that the Senator flights were created purely as a prestige service to distinguish the airline. It was the Senator, gauged to the movement of business traffic to and from Central Europe, that established Lufthansa's superior service in the public consciousness. The Senator Service was a rousing success from the beginning, even in competition with jet aircraft already introduced by other North Atlantic carriers. It was so successful, in fact, that Lufthansa made the Senator its new standard First Class service, incorporating it on the South Atlantic and Far East routes, the latter featuring an Oriental stewardess extra to the regular crew.

During 1959 Lufthansa included Milan, Athens, Barcelona, Stockholm, Geneva, Manchester, and Nice in its European route structure, and in November reestablished its Far East route as far as Bangkok via Cairo, Karachi and Calcutta. This run was operated twice weekly with Super Constellation equipment. Also that year Lufthansa occupied its present North American Divisional Headquarters on three floors of 410 Park Avenue. President Eisenhower's Peace Medal was awarded to Lufthansa in July, 1959, for the airline's important contribution to the understanding and free exchange of ideas between the people of West Germany and the United States. This was a great honor for the airline, it being the only such award presented to a foreign air carrier. Lufthansa was again cited by the People-to-People Committee in June, 1961, this time under the administration of President Kennedy, for the airline's participation in the town affiliation program of the overall People-to-People Program.

1960 was Lufthansa's year of the jet. The airline started off in February by ordering a fifth Boeing 707 Intercontinental and four intermediate-range Boeing 720-B's. On March 17, the first Boeing 707 jet flight from New York non-stop to Frankfurt spanned the North Atlantic in a fraction of the time consumed by the record-setting catapult flight of 30 years earlier. The inaugural jet flight from Frankfurt to San Francisco took place on May 16, simultaneously bringing Montreal into the Lufthansa jet network. Distance on this run, with a stop in Paris, is approximately 6500 miles. The Frankfurt-Chicago jet service was introduced two days later, on May 18, operating initially via Paris, later non-stop. Both the Chicago and San Francisco jet operation were set up initially as a twice-weekly service, the New York operation a daily service. Seating on the flights was on a dual configuration basis, with both Senator and Economy sections. On November 22, 1960, indicating the effect of the jets, Lufthansa carried its one millionth passenger for the year, by the end of December had carried 1,237,629 passengers. Lufthansa ordered four more Boeing 720-B's in November, thus finishing up this memorable year on the proper note.

Jets replaced the twice-weekly flights on the Far East route January 23, 1961, and the route itself was extended to Hong Kong and Tokyo. Dhahran, Saudi Arabia, had been added to this route the previous August. As deliveries on the first four Boeing 720-B's began in the spring of 1961, they were integrated into the existing jet network, and introduced on the South Atlantic run May 20, operating twice-weekly. The airline in July 1961 put jets on the Middle East service from Frankfurt to Teheran via Munich, Vienna, Beirut and Baghdad. Lufthansa placed an order for twelve short-to-medium range Boeing 727 jets at the end of February, 1961. Due for delivery during 1964/65, these aircraft were scheduled for integration into the European and Near East networks. A new destination, Ankara, Turkey, was added to the Near East route in April.

An interesting advance of the airline during 1961 was the purchase in March of a small German air carrier called **Condor Luftreederei of Hamburg.** Lufthansa

F-36 was faster, improved version of F-22, carrying thirty two at 165 mph.

gained two Convair 440 Metropolitans by this move, but more important, the purchase calls to mind the name of Lufthansa's predecessor over 40 years earlier, which was **Deutsche Luftreederei.** This was the most active airline in Germany prior to the formation of the German Aero Lloyd, the first big combine of the many small mail and passenger carriers operating in that country between 1918 and 1923. The purchase of Condor Luftreederei in 1961 in a way marks the completion of a cycle in German aviation and the development of Lufthansa German Airlines.

A quick look at Lufthansa's record since resumption of service in 1955 shows that the airline set a dynamic pace for itself. The airline doubled and redoubled its operation on every front, as proved by the following figures:

(1) A jet fleet either delivered or on order totalling 25 aircraft, with indications of further purchases in the very near future.

(2) A further increase of the company's capital to DM 250 millions from the previous high of DM 180 millions. (Lufthansa, incidentally is still approximately 80% government owned.)

(3) An increase in total passengers carried from 74,000 the first year (actually eight months of 1955) to 786,000 in 1959, to 1,237,000 in 1960.

(4) Network mileage increase from 8051 miles in 1955 to 55,750 in 1961.

(5) Increase in number of employees worldwide from 2040 in 1955 to over 10,000 in 1961, roughly 1000 of these in the North American Division.

(6) 550 tons of cargo carried in 1955 compared to 16,370 tons in 1960.

(7) Lufthansa fleet increased from 11 aircraft in 1955 to 32 in 1959, will number at least 70 by the time the Boeing 727's are delivered in 1964/65.

Fleet breakdown as follows:

  12 Boeing 727
   8 Boeing 720-B
   5 Boeing 707
   9 Vickers Viscount
  11 Convair 440's
   7 Lockheed 1049-G Super Constellations
   2 Lockheed 1649 Super Star Constellations
   2 Lockheed 1649-Er Super Constellations
     converted to cargo
  14 Training aircraft

Lufthansa consistently bettered its monthly, quarterly and yearly figures during this short six-year period. The airline constructed at the extensive Frankfurt facility a large modern commissary and flight kitchen now preparing upwards of 6000 meals daily. This is part of a Lufthansa "city" which has taken shape in the last few years in an area adjacent to the Frankfurt airport. This area includes a new modern administration building containing the worldwide operations headquarters; a huge suspension type jet hangar for on-line maintenance of the jet fleet; a large modern cafeteria in the hangar for employee use; a heating plant designed after the glass-fronted heating and air conditioning plant at New York's Idlewild Airport; and a pilot training center containing Flight Simulators for the Boeing 707, Super Constellation, and Vickers Viscount, each able to reproduce exactly all the normal and abnormal conditions of flight in these aircraft. It was with the Boeing Flight Simulator that Lufthansa pilots plotted and "flew" tactical missions with the Boeing 707 for a full year before the first jet aircraft was delivered.

Lufthansa now maintains a cargo schedule across the North Atlantic alone capable of moving over a million tons of cargo monthly between North America and Europe. Estimates have been made by company officials that by 1970 Lufthansa will draw up to 50% of its revenue from the cargo business, which has developed rapidly since 1955 alongside the passenger operation.

Lufthansa's meteoric success since 1955 is indicative of the determination and careful planning that helped make possible the economic recovery of the Federal Republic of Germany under the Marshall Plan. The characteristic German traits of meticulousness, thoroughness and pride in work well done show in all phases of the airline: in the skill of its pilots; in its distinguished flight service; in its smooth running ground operation, from maintenance and overhaul to answering a telephone or writing a ticket. The airline today reflects the same strength, skill and imagination, that originally established it years ago as one of aviation's outstanding pioneers.

In U.S.A. Air cooled radial engines and monocoque fuselage design sent transport trends in another direction. Continental Airlines Lockheed *Vega* is prime example.

Lockheed *Vega* carried five, cruised at 170 mph for Braniff Airways.

Northrop *Delta* was glamour plane of TWA fleet in early '30's, cruising at over 200 mph with eight passengers.

TWA carried both mail and passengers in Lockheed Orions from 1933 to 1935.

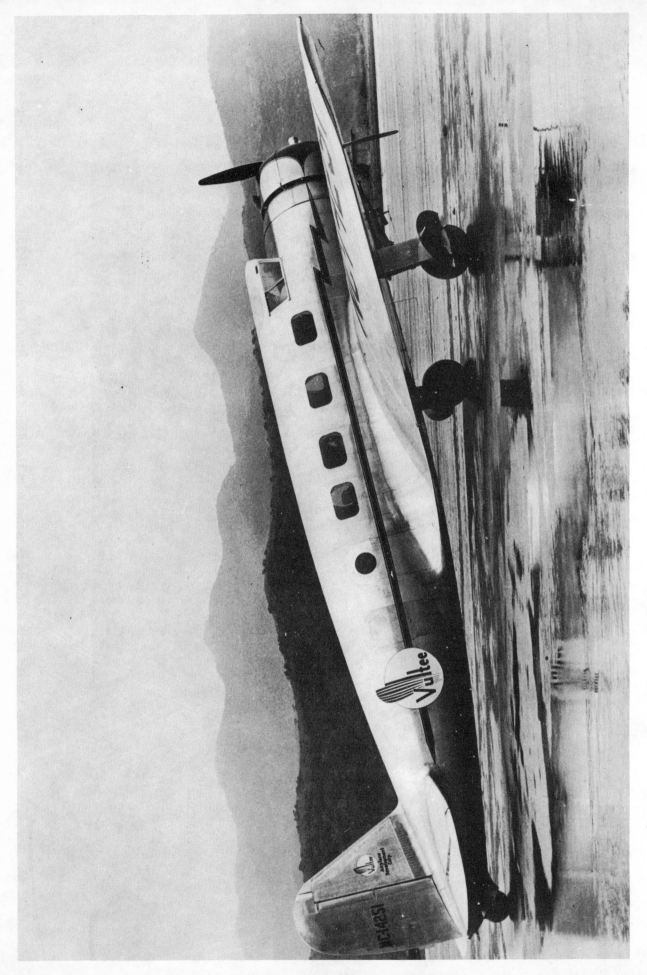

Vultee V-1 used by American Airlines was one of fastest early-30's transports, at 211 mph cruising speed. Later it was re-designed into the V-11 attack-bomber.

NORTHWEST ORIENT AIRLINES

THE HISTORY of Northwest Orient Airlines is one of pioneering over rugged mountains and vast oceans — and of the development of an international carrier from a small, regional airmail route.

The second-oldest air carrier in the United States with a continuous identification, Northwest began operations October 1, 1926, as an airmail carrier between Minneapolis/St. Paul and Chicago.

The Company was incorporated August 1, 1926, as Northwest Airways, a Michigan corporation. It was backed financially by businessmen of Detroit and Minneapolis/St. Paul. Control later shifted to the Twin Cities group.

Northwest inaugurated passenger service in July, 1927. Service continued for three months before it was suspended for the winter. In 1927, the Company carried 106 passengers.

In 1928, Northwest Airways began the route expansion that saw it develop in 20 years into Northwest Orient Airlines one of the world's largest domestic and international airlines that now carries more than two million passengers yearly.

From 1928 through 1933 NWA expanded westward, city by city, through the Dakotas, Montana and Washington State.

Northwest Orient Airlines now serves a 20,000-mile route system stretching from New York/Newark and Baltimore/Washington, D.C. across the northern tier of states to Portland and Seattle/Tacoma. It also serves a domestic route between the Upper Mid-West and the southeastern cities of Atlanta, Ga., and Tampa, St. Petersburg, Clearwater, Fort Lauderdale and Miami, Florida.

Northwest's "overseas" and international routes serve Honolulu, Hawaii and Anchorage, Alaska, and the cities of Winnipeg and Edmonton, Canada. It operates over the North Pacific "Great Circle" route from Seattle/Tacoma to Tokyo, Seoul, Taipei, Okinawa and Manila. It also operates a Polar Imperial route from New York to Anchorage to the Orient.

Since its inception, Northwest has grown from within, expanding its route system in an orderly and logical manner, without taking part in an airline merger.

Northwest's route expansion through the northern areas — Canada, Alaska and the Aleutian Islands — came after World War II although Croil Hunter, long-time pioneering president of NWA and now its Board Chairman, visualized a "Northwest Passage" to the Orient in the early 1930's.

(The "Great Circle" route across the Pacific flown by Northwest is considerably shorter than the mid-Pacific route because it is far north of the earth's equatorial bulge. From New York City to Hong Kong, for instance, is 9,245 miles via the Great Circle, 11,154 miles via the mid-Pacific).

Because of Northwest's experience flying northern transcontinental routes, the United States government called on Northwest at the onset of World War II to set up and operate a military cargo route to Canada, Alaska and the Aleutians.

With military C-46's and C-47's Northwest's pilots flew more than 21 million miles with a performance factor better than that of many airlines operating domestically at the time.

Four Northwest pilots were awarded Air Medals by the President of the United States for their contributions to the war effort and to aviation while flying this Northern Region operation.

Northwest's experience in this area during the war was taken into account by the Civil Aeronautics Board when NWA's Orient routes were granted and the vision of a "Northwest Passage" to the Orient became reality.

Northwest made other notable contributions to the war effort. It set up and operated a bomber modification plant in St. Paul, Minnesota, and another at Vandalia, Ohio. Thousands of B-25 and B-26 bombers were flown directly from manufacturing plants to these modification centers and outfitted for "cold weather" operation in northern areas of the world. Bombers modified at Northwest's bases were among the first to bomb the Kiel and Ploesti oil fields, and they pulverized enemy defenses in Normandy on D-day. Northwest also cooperated with the Air Force in several vital projects, among them research into plane icing, communications static and high-altitude flying.

Because of Northwest's experience flying the short Great Circle route across the Pacific, the Air Force in 1950 called on Northwest to be a prime contractor in the operation of the now famous Korean Airlift which began shortly after the Korean war broke out in June of that year.

Flying DC-4 aircraft, Northwest completed 1,380 Korean Airlift round-trip trans-Pacific crossings — a total of more than 13 million miles — before its part in the airlift was completed. During this period Northwest flew 40,000 soldiers and 12 million pounds of high-priority military cargo — from bomber engines to medical supplies — across the Pacific Ocean.

This was done with no disruption to Northwest's regular commercial schedule of trans-Pacific flights.

Northwest crews, based in Tokyo, also operated "UN-99" a United Nations DC-3, which carried a UN observer team to Allied positions in South Korea during the fighting.

Northwest started operations in 1926 with two rented planes, an OX-5 Curtiss Oriole and an OX-5 Thomas Morse, both open cockpit jobs. Its first "fleet" consisted of three 85 mile-an-hour Stinson "Detroiters." They carried three passengers and were so named because they were designed by Eddie Stinson and built in the Motor City. They were the first closed-cabin planes used by an American commercial airline.

"Detroiters" were followed by the all-metal Hamilton high-wing monoplane, the Ford Tri-Motor (advertised as the plane with "windows that open and close and complete lavatory facilities"): the Waco J-6; Travelaire 6000; Lockheed Orion; Lockheed 10A (Electra); Lockheed 14H (Zephyr); a Siskorsky Amphibian (used between airports in the Twin Cities and the Duluth, Minnesota, boat harbor); the Douglas DC-3; Douglas

Heinkel *HE-70* was fast German 'intimate' transport used by Lufthansa.

DC-4; Martin 202; Boeing B-377; Douglas DC-6B; Lockheed 1049G Super Constellation; Douglas DC-7C; Lockheed L-188 prop-jet, Douglas DC-8C and the latest, the Boeing 720B turbo-fan medium jet airliner.

In 1954, Donald W. Nyrop was named president of Northwest Orient Airlines. Mr. Nyrop replaced Gen. Harold R. Harris who held that position briefly. Croil Hunter, NWA president for 15 years previous to the advent of Gen. Harris, still serves as Board Chairman.

Mr. Nyrop is a native of Elgin, Nebraska and was graduated from Doane College, Crete, Nebraska in 1934. He taught high school at Humboldt, Nebraska during the school year 1934-1935.

In 1935 he went to Washington, D.C. to study law at George Washington University. He reecived his L.L.B degree from that school in 1939. While attending Law school he worked as an auditor in the government's General Accounting office.

In October, 1939, he became an attorney in the General Counsel's office of the Civil Aeronautics Authority. On January 1, 1942, he was named special assistant to the chairman of the Civil Aeronautics Board.

He served with the Army Air Force from August, 1942 until January, 1946, being stationed in Washington as executive officer for operations of the Air Transport Command. He left the service with the rank of Lieutenant Colonel.

In 1946 Mr. Nyrop joined the Air Transport Association of America. He represented the carriers of this organization as a member of the official United States delegations at the International Civil Aviation Organization operations conferences in 1946 and 1947.

In July, 1948, Mr. Nyrop returned to government service as deputy administrator of the Civil Aeronautics Administration. By Presidential appointment, he served as Administrator of the Civil Aeronautics Administration in 1950 and 1951.

He became chairman of the Civil Aeronautics Board in April, 1951, and remained in this position until October, 1952. In January, 1953, he joined the law firm of Klagsbrunn, Hanes and Irwin as a partner. It was from this private law practice that he came to Northwest Orient Airlines.

Important dates in Northwest's route expansion:

June 1, 1945: Northwest became the nation's fourth transcontinental airline when service was extended eastward from the Twin Cities to Newark and New York City via Milwaukee and Detroit.

Aug. 1, 1946: Northwest was certificated to fly to the Far East via the short "Great Circle" route.

Sept. 1, 1946: Northwest began operating into Anchorage, Alaska, via the "outside" route up the Canadian and Alaska coasts from Seattle/Tacoma.

Jan. 2, 1947: Service to Anchorage began via the "inside" route from the Twin Cities across northwestern Canada, with Edmonton, Alberta, a fuel stop.

July 15, 1947: Scheduled service began to the Orient. Stops included Anchorage, Tokyo, Seoul, Shanghai, Okinawa and Manila.

March 15, 1948: Service was extended to Washington, D.C., from Detroit via Cleveland and Pittsburgh.

Dec. 2, 1948: Northwest began service to Honolulu, Hawaii, from Seattle/Tacoma and Portland. Northwest was the first airline certificated to link Hawaii with the Pacific Northwest.

April 30, 1950: Edmonton, Alberta, became a passenger stop on the "inside" route to Alaska and the Orient.

June 30, 1950: Northwest extended its service to the Chinese Nationalist island of Formosa (Taiwan).

Oct. 30, 1955: Northwest began direct service between Chicago and New York.

Dec. 6, 1958: Service inaugurated to Tampa/St. Petersburg/Clearwater and Miami, Florida from the Upper Midwest.

Sept. 27, 1959: Service inaugurated to Atlanta, Georgia.

Jan. 1, 1960: Service inaugurated to Fort Lauderdale, Florida.

Dec. 15, 1960: Service inaugurated to Baltimore, Maryland.

First "really modern" American transport (1933) which was to set pattern for world, was Boeing 247 (247-D shown) carrying ten at 165 mph cruising speed.

Potez 62, flying for Air France, had six passenger capacity, cruised at 173 mph.

Douglas DC-2, considered 'tricky' ship to fly by many pilots, made good reputation for Douglas company.

DC-2's ranged far and wide. Swissair Douglas carried fourteen cruised at 190 mph.

QANTAS DC-2 "Bungana" was first all-metal commercial aircraft used in Australia.

PAN AMERICAN WORLD AIRWAYS

MODERN CIVILIZATION in the broad sense came to Latin America on caravels during the Golden Age of Explorers — Columbus, Cortez, Pizarro and their like — but it really took the air age to unlock the rich storehouse that daring had discovered.

A popular and colorful catch-phrase has it that quite a few Latin American lands turned, in transportation, directly from the burro to the airplane. Unlike many catch-phrases, this one is exactly true.

In many places in Latin America even today, oxcarts draw up on airfields to unload their burdens directly into the cargo compartments of winged wagons.

All over the southern half of this hemisphere, airplanes are providing a safe and dependable form of transportation where virtually no other forms exist. They are serving as farm trucks, ambulances, school buses, furniture vans and mine wagons, among other things.

And it was a United States flag airline, Pan American World Airways, that did much of the pioneering to unlock a continent, establish a new concept of the role of aviation in world commerce, and give the United States one of the world's greatest international air carriers.

The huge, 575-mile-an-hour Boeing and Douglas jet-liners, delivered to Pan American before any other airline in the world, are going far toward realizing the long standing dream of Juan T. Trippe, Pan American's first and only president, of the airliner as an instrument of mass transportation. He predicts the jetliners, carrying from 120 to 189 passengers, will double international air travel.

"Air transport has a choice — a very clear choice — of becoming a luxury service to carry the well-to-do at high prices or to carry the average man at what he can afford to pay," says Trippe. "Pan American has chosen the latter course."

It is in line with that policy that Pan American in 1948 became the world's first scheduled airline to offer low-cost tourist service, and followed that up with even lower "thrift" class service.

Mass travel by air, Trippe believes, may prove to be more significant to world destiny than the atom bomb.

"The tourist plane and the bomber for years have been racing each other toward a photo finish," he says. "In my opinion, however, the tourist plane, if allowed to move forward unshackled by political boundaries and economic restrictions, will win this race between education and catastrophe."

The accelerating progress of the plane toward the mass transportation stage is clearly shown in the records written by Pan American.

The airline that was born on a Key West mudflat with one eight-passenger airplane and seven employees today has some 22,000 employees with 150 four-engine jet and piston Clippers flying 66,700 miles of round-the-world routes.

The story of Pan American is a story of high adventure, daring, pioneering, faith, and progress compounded sometimes by sheer genius and again by homely improvisation.

In the history of international aviation, the broad-winged Clippers of Pan American stand as Twentieth Century versions of the Conestoga wagons with which America's pioneers pushed across the wild, unmapped plains of the West and opened up a whole continent.

Much of the Pan American story has been written in Latin America, where it was born on October 28, 1927, and where it flexed its fledgling wings before going on to conquer the Pacific in 1935, the Atlantic in 1939, and finally, in 1947, to become the world's first round-the-world airline.

From a humble beginning with a 90-mile route between Key West, Florida, and Havana, Cuba, the Pan Am System now flies to 82 lands all over the world — 34 in Latin America alone.

In the early days, Latin America was a gigantic problem that challenged the vision, daring and pioneering of President Trippe and the men he gathered around him.

The combination of rugged terrain cut with mountains, valleys and tangled jungles in many Latin Countries, vast distances, especially in South America, and sparsely settled interiors had hampered Latin America's communications over the centuries. The airplane offered the first solution to the problem that had daunted everything but surefooted burros and mountain goats.

Before the air age, most Latin American capitals were weeks away from the United States and even each other via slow steamer service. In many cases, Europe actually was closer to South America than was the United States. A resident of Caracas had to travel to New York to catch a ship for Rio de Janeiro.

Today, most major cities in Latin America are only a few hours from the United States and each other by 575-mile-an-hour jet Clippers.

This change did not come easily. Pan American's air pioneers shed their full quota of blood and sweat and tears — and then some.

For some 15 years prior to World War II, Pan Am acted much as a second State Department of the United States as it blazed air trails across previously impassable jungles and once-indomitable mountains.

Landing rights had to be negotiated directly with foreign governments to establish airports, and then sweating Pan American engineers and crews had to carve them by hand out of jungles and mountain-rimmed plateaus. Pan American had to set up its own communications and weather reporting systems.

Pan American engineers helped design planes specifically for the long overwater hops, the jungle airports and other peculiar problems faced in international operations. New techniques had to be developed and personnel trained for overwater flying and ocean navigation.

Many of the survey flights mapping the new routes for the pioneer U.S. flag international airline during the 1930's were made by the world-famed transatlantic solo flier, Charles A. Lindbergh.

Pan American became largely the instrument for

Douglas DC-3 is one of the most famous and long-lived aircraft in the world. First used in 1936, it is still in service of many carriers.

bringing the air age to all the major lands of Latin America. The Pan American system today is serving Antigua, Argentina, Bahamas, Barbados, Bolivia, Brazil, British Guiana, British Honduras, Chile, Cuba, Curacao, Colombia, Costa Rica, Dominican Republic, Ecuador, El Salvador, French Guiana, Guadeloupe, Guatemala, Haiti, Honduras, Jamaica, Martinique, Mexico, Nicaragua, Paraguay, Peru, Puerto Rico, Panama, Surinam, Trinidad, Uruguay, Venezuela and the Virgin Islands.

More than 400 scheduled passenger flights and more than 70 all-cargo flights weekly are operated between the United States and these countries by Pan American.

Diplomats, businessmen, students and tourists are constantly shuttling back and forth between the Americas, building an ever-stronger community of interests. Cargo planes wing southward with everything from baby chicks to refrigerators, delivering orders in hours instead of days. They make their return trips loaded with strategic materials, coffee, bananas and dozens of other products from the Latin lands.

In pioneering the Latin American air trails, Pan American racked up a substantial number of the many "firsts" it has written into American transport aviation history.

Pan American was the first to operate a permanent international air service, first to operate regular foreign airmail service, to utilize radio in air transport, to develop an airways traffic control system, to develop and use instrument flying techniques, to develop a complete aviation weather service, to develop and operate four-engines flying boats, operate four-engine landplanes, operate low-cost tourist type air service, and many others.

One of its most significant achievements was to forge the longest nonstop overwater flight regularly operated anywhere in the world when it opened the 600-mile route between Kingston, Jamaica, and the Panama Canal Zone on December 2, 1930.

This Caribbean basin was the laboratory where Pan American learned the skills in ocean navigation and overwater flying that enabled its masters of ocean flying to go on to conquer the vast reaches of the Pacific and Atlantic.

When World War II broke out, Pan American put its planes, personnel and know-how at the service of the government. One task assigned Pan Am in the war effort was to establish and operate the 11,500-mile "Cannonball" run of the Africa-Orient service from Miami to India. War supplies and important personnel flew out; the wounded, returning combat veterans and prisoners of war flew back.

Pan American also ferried more than 1,100 bombers via the South Atlantic to Europe, and when the Japs cut the Burma road, Pan Am personnel flew men and supplies "over the hump" of the Himalayas from India to provide a lifeline to China.

The company also was given the tremendous wartime undertaking of building more than 50 airports in 15 different countries of the world.

Pan American's contributions to the defense of the free world did not end with World War II.

It took part in the Berlin Airlift that kept the German capital alive when the Soviets clamped their blockade on the city. It organized a 6,700-mile Pacific Airlift

during the Korean emergency, with as many as six airlines integrating flight operations. It operates and maintains the Guided Missiles Range at Cape Canaveral, Florida, for the Department of Defense, including the manning of tracking stations set up on a string of islands down through the Caribbean and South Atlantic.

The epic of aerial pioneering written by Pan American in the Latin American field not only benefited United States' neighbors to the south through enhanced international trade and cultural interchange. The airline also embarked early on a program of fostering the development of domestic airlines within the countries it served.

Over the years, Pan American has helped organize and invested in 12 national airlines in 11 Latin American countries. It still has a minority interest in 10 of these affiliates, in Brazil, Colombia, Costa Rica, Honduras, Mexico, Nicaragua, Venezuela, Panama and Bolivia.

In addition, Pan American's aviation know-how and experience has been called to the aid of aviation in other parts of the world. Outstanding technical assistance programs were set up by Pan American in cooperation with the U.S. government's International Cooperation Administration to help expand and develop the air transport systems of Turkey, Pakistan, Thailand and Afghanistan.

In fostering these domestic airlines Pan American in a number of countries contributed substantially to creating an entire new industry and avocation — air transport. Pan Am technicians and training facilities were devoted to teaching airline and aircraft maintenance to truck drivers, garage mechanics and others. Local residents were taught to operate control towers, to perform traffic functions, to man radio stations and to become experts in sales procedures.

Friendly relations have been built between a U.S. company and government officials and businessmen in other lands, effectively combating "Yankee Imperialism" propaganda.

Thanks largely to the new fields — geographic and economic — opened by the air transport industry, United States trade has been greatly enhanced. Nowhere is this more true than in Latin America. In the past quarter of a century, Latin American trade has virtually quadrupled. And the trend there has been diverted from Europe to the United States.

In 1931, the first year Pan American was in the cargo business, some 4,000 pounds of Latin American cargo was handled. Today, that's less than a half a load for just one of Pan American's fleet of busy cargo Clippers.

At the same time, Clipper cargo rates have been reduced constantly, enabling more and more shippers to take advantage of this quick, simple and money-saving form of transportation. The average ton-mile cost of Clipper cargo shipments today is less than one-third what it was only about 10 years ago.

The figures are rapidly bearing out the prediction made recently by Pan Am Executive Vice President Wilbur L. Morrison, in charge of the Latin American Division, that within 10 years, cargo revenues in the Latin American Division would exceed passenger revenues.

KLM's DC-3's ranged far from Los Angeles, California where they were built through the mid-30's.

On snow covered runway, workhorse DC-3 waits to take off for Canadian Pacific DC-3's were designed for twenty four passengers, have carried up to sixty!

Lockheed all-metal low wing twin engined transport entry in '30's was 10-A, shown here in Trans-Canada Airlines markings.

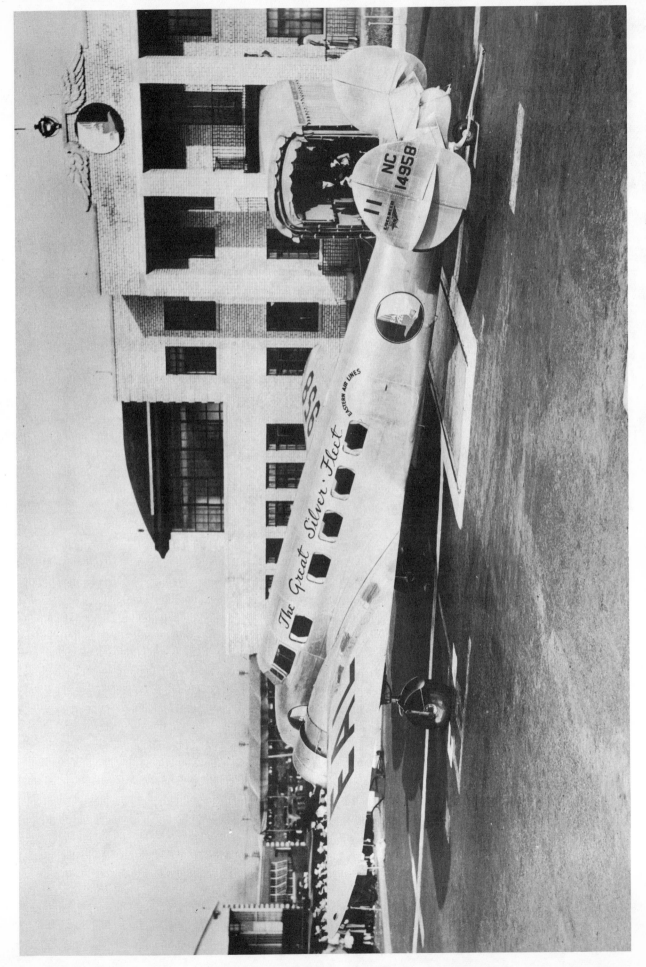

Eastern Airlines purchased fleet of Lockheed 10-A's when Capt. Eddie Rickenbacker modernized the line, offered fast service to Florida.

Lockheed 14, here in Northwest Airlines trim, flew eleven passengers at 200 mph.

QANTAS EMPIRE AIRWAYS LIMITED

THERE IS A wealth of romance in the 41-years history of Australia's overseas airline Qantas — 41 years that make it one of the world's oldest established airlines.

It is the story of growth from a 577-mile air route between two small bush towns in the North Australian hinterland to 63,000 unduplicated route miles and a round-the-world jet service.

From a "fleet" of two tiny, 60 m.p.h., 100-horsepower World War 1 biplanes to a fleet that includes eleven 600 m.p.h., 110-ton, 50,000 horsepower turbofan-powered Boeing 707 V-Jet airlines, four Electra Turboprops, and many other aircraft.

From flying 3,000 miles in two years to flying 18 million miles a year; from flying a first million miles in 10 years to flying a million miles every three weeks.

From a staff of three to a staff of 7,000 and from a one-room, weatherboard "head office" in a small country town to a 16-floor head office in Sydney, and branch offices all over the world.

From a company with a total paid-up capital of $16,963.97 to a company with $50,580,000 capital, assets of $177,030,000 and revenue of $95,540,000 a year.

This is the growth bridged by the 41 years history of Qantas.

The story begins with an old "Tin Lizzie" car shaking and rattling over impossible country in Australia's northern outback. Drivers of the protesting car were two young ex-world War 1 Flying Corps Lieutenants, W. Hudson Fysh and P. J. McGinness, who had been commissioned by the Australian Government to survey an air route between northern Australian towns of Longreach and Darwin.

Between rattles and bumps, the two young airmen, contrasting their recent flying experiences with this slow and bone-rattling method of travel, envisioned an aerial service as the answer to the problem of outback travel.

A chance meeting between the airmen and a grazier named Fergus McMaster, whose car they rescued when it was bogged in a sandy river bed, led to the foundation of Qantas. McMaster shared their enthusiasm for an outback air service. He and grazier friends raised the money which enabled them to register "Queensland and Northern Territory Aerial Services" as a company in November 1920. Almost immediately this rather unwieldy name was popularly abbreviated to Qantas.

Soon the new air service was operating — with two war-type biplanes capable of 60 M.P.H. and a total staff of three consisting of an engineer named Arthur Baird and pilots McGinness and Hudson Fysh.

During 1921 and 1922 the new airline flew some 3,000 miles and carried 871 passengers, mainly on joy rides. Seventy-nine taxi flights were also chartered during this period, one being the first maternity case in Australia to be taken to hospital by air, while another was the first recorded aerial turkey-shooting expedition.

The first regular air service began on November 2, 1922 — between the towns of Charleville and Clon-curry. This 577 mile trip was considered too far to fly in one day because of the inland heat, so there was an overnight stop at Longreach where Qantas then had its head office. Today, one of Qantas' Boeing 707 jets could fly this first air route in little more than one hour.

The payload on the historic first flight was 400 lb. (maximum payload for a Boeing 707 is 34,000 lbs.) and 108 letters were carried. The first passenger was 85-year old Alexander Kennedy who 53 years earlier had pioneered the route by bullock-wagon, taking eight months for the trip. In the first year of regular services Qantas carried 208 passengers.

The Qantas fleet began to grow with the addition in 1923 of a DeHavilland-4 converted war-type machine and, later, two DH9C aircraft. The latter were considered very much the "last word", as they boasted a noise-reduced cabin (virtually a cockpit with a simple lid) and passengers were able to dispense with the customary cap and goggles.

Almost every year since then has marked some milestone in the growth of Qantas and Australian aviation history. The first ground-to-air radio experiments in 1925 — since when Qantas has always kept right abreast of any developments in radio for aviation purposes. The first commercial aircraft (a DH50) to be built in Australia in 1926, and in the same year the company's first flying school opened at Longreach. Another flying school at Brisbane in 1927. The world's first Flying Doctor service organized by the Australian Inland Mission in 1928 and operated by Qantas for the next 21 years. In the same year Australia's first daily air-service — between Brisbane and Toowoomba.

The first step in the transistion of Qantas from a domestic to an overseas airline was taken in 1931 when the company participated in the carriage of the first experimental airmails.

In 1934 the company was registered as "Qantas Empire Airways Limited", the first word of the new company name incorporating the initials of the pioneer company.

Then began a unique aerial partnership which is still going strong today after a quarter of a century. The first regular Australia-England started in 1934 when Qantas in conjunction with Imperial Airways (forerunner of BOAC) began flying what was to become the "Kangaroo Route" from England to Australia through India — the longest air service in the world.

It began with a schedule of one service per week. Qantas was responsible for the Brisbane-Singapore sector. Total time for the 12,000 — odd miles journey was 12 to 14 days — considered then quite remarkable.

Next step was the introduction of flying boats to this service in 1938.

The flying boat service was a great step forward in international air travel. The flying boats, with full course meal service, plenty of room to move about, and even sleeping accommodation, ushered in totally new standards of comfort for air travellers.

With the outbreak of war in 1939 the England-Australia service became a vital line of communications

Trans-Canada was using sleek Lockheed 14's in 1940 at outbreak of WWII.

and through the war years, although normal international traffic was brought to a halt, Qantas operated on a fast-expanding, if unconventional, scale.

Qantas took over operation of the Australia service as far as Karachi. And round the same time Qantas gained its first experience of trans-pacific flying when it undertook the task of ferrying 19 Catalina flying boats from America to Australia for the Commonwealth Government.

Then, when enemy advance interrupted the Australia service, Qantas embarked on one of the more remarkable chapters of its history when it bridged the gap by flying a service from Perth in Western Australia to Colombo nonstop across 3513 miles of Indian Ocean.

This world record distance was operated originally by Catalinas each carrying a 3¼ ton overload of fuel, flying in complete radio silence with no radio navigation aids and little weather information, and taking from 27 to 31 hours for the crossing.

Catalinas gave way to Liberators, Liberators to Lancastrians. When it was all over Qantas had made 824 of those Indian Ocean crossings. From these flights Qantas developed a unique long-range operations technique which was to be the solid foundation of its postwar expansion. Three Qantas pilots largely responsible for the Indian Ocean Services — Captains Crowther, Tapp and Ambrose — won the Johnston Memorial Air Navigation Trophy, most coveted international award.

Since the war, using first converted wartime bombers and then gradually acquiring postwar commercial aircraft, Qantas has had its biggest expansion. Almost every year has seen the opening of new services. A new direct service to Japan, Noumea, and Suva, New Guinea, Hong Kong, Colombo, Bombay, Djakarta, Beirut, Athens, Frankfurt, South Africa, North America, and finally the world's first direct round-the-globe service.

In 1954 Qantas took over operation of the Commonwealth Pacific Airlines service to the United States and Canada. Deliveries of Super Constellations had begun and the new Qantas trans-Pacific service was inaugurated when "Southern Constellation" departed Sydney on May 15.

The year 1958 saw the ratification of the agreement between Australia and the United States under which Qantas is permitted to operate across the American continent through San Francisco and New York and on across the Atlantic to the United Kingdom and Europe.

The Round-The-World service — the world's first — began in January 1958 when two Super Constellations departed Melbourne — one flying east across the United States to London and the other flying west through India.

Now with a route mileage exceeding 62,000 miles and flying more than 18,000,000 miles a year, Qantas is well launched into the Jet age. Her fleet of eleven Boeing 707s now fly Qantas' round-the-world route from Sydney through Singapore, Bangkok, Calcutta, Karachi, Cairo, Rome, New York, San Francisco, Honolulu and Fiji back to Sydney.

These Boeings are the turbofan-powered V-Jets, the fastest and most up-to-date commercial jet aircraft in operation. They are used also for the Qantas Far East service to Tokyo through Manila and Hong Kong and another service between Australia and Noumea.

Qantas propjet Electras fly many trans-Tasman services linking Sydney and Melbourne with principal New Zealand cities Wellington, Auckland and Christchurch, while the Qantas Wallaby Route service spans the vastness of the Indian Ocean, operating between Australia and South Africa through Cocos Island and Mauritius to Johannesburg.

For the businessman or tourist, Qantas jet services bring the rest of the world to within flying time measured only in hours.

Lodestar was Lockheed ultimate refinement of 10-A design. It was capable of above 250 mph. cruising speeds, carried fifteen.

Swissair Junkers JU-86 twin engined transports (1936) were quite fast at 224 mph cruising with ten passengers.

Unique Douglas DC-5 was used by KLM in Europe. Capacity: sixteen.

Famed Pan American "Clipper" designations began with these Sikorsky S-42's which transported thirty two passengers to far parts of the globe.

Amphib and seaplane development continued in U.S. but at slower rate than land transport planes. This Pan American Sikorsky S-43 served in Caribbean.

Martin 130 "China Clipper" (over San Francisco's Golden Gate) extended Pan American's web to Orient with more speed and greater comfort for fifty passengers.

Last of the big flying boats, Pan Am's "Atlantic Clipper", Boeing 314 carried eighty nine at 175 mph.

SABENA BELGIAN WORLD AIRLINES

ESTABLISHED IN 1923 on the initiative of SNETA (Societe Nationale pour l'Etude des Transports Ariens), and financed jointly by public and private capital, SABENA has for well over thirty years been successfully responsible for Belgian air transport. SABENA's history dates back to before commercial aviation. It shows a brilliant record of constant progress and development. Thanks to the Belgian air lines, Belgium is represented today not only all over Europe and in Africa, but also in the Middle East and the United States. In all parts of the world the name SABENA spells progress, reliability and conscientious performance, the results of which bear fruit daily.

Hardly had the first world war ended but Belgium saw the vast possibilities of aviation with King Albert, so aptly called "The Airman King'" in the front rank. With the King's help SNETA was formed into a company on March 1, 1919 by M. Albert Marchall and a group of go-ahead businessmen. The chief initiator of this enterprise was Flight Lieutenant Georges Nelis, with his associates Jean Renard, Henri Cornelius and Tony Orta, all young veterans of the 1914-18 Belgian Airforce.

These pioneers examined the possibilities of air lines in Europe and the Belgian Congo, and experimental flights were made between Brussels, Paris and Amsterdam. The inauguration of the first 360-mile air route took place in July 1920 between Leopoldville, the capital of the Belgian Congo and N'Gombe further up the River Congo.

Belgian wings therefore, were the first to fly in the African sky where they have been ever since. With ever-increasing success they continue to bear witness to the vitality and the economic and social progress of Belgium.

From then on LARA (Ligne Aerienne Roi Albert) progressed rapidly. In 1921 the line was extended to Lisala (744 miles), and subsequently to Stanleyville (1,078 miles), and it was flown with perfect regularity by SNETA hydroplanes carrying mail, freight and passengers. Later the African sky "squatters" set about establishing hundreds of aerodromes and emergency runways, thus enabling the young Belgian wings to penetrate even further into the heart of the virgin forest.

Experimental flights were followed by those of postal aircraft in Europe, and the aerial carriage of mail soon became a habit. SNETA having completed its work of prospection up to this point, with the help of the Belgian State and its Colony, SABENA (Societe Anonyme Belge d'Exploitation de la Navigation Aerienne) then took over the task of organizing Belgium's commercial airlines.

The first official flight took place on May 23, 1923, when a single-engined De Havilland carried mail and goods from Brussels via Ostend to Lympne. From that day until the outbreak of the second world war the development of SABENA ran side by side with the advance made in technical and commercial aviation throughout the world, relating directly to Belgium's economic expansion.

Twin-engined planes were slowly replaced by, in the first instance, three-engined Handley Pages and Fokkers, needed for stepping up the cruising speeds from 75 m.p.h. to 103 m.p.h. and subsequently by Savoia-Marchetti S-73's and S-83's which later won for Belgium the Blue Riband of transcontinental flights. The first twin-engined DC-3's were delivered in 1939.

SABENA realized before long the great importance and potentialities of air freight. This led, in 1925, to the transporting of, among other goods, racing pigeons to northern and central France. SABENA soon added to its list, which already included Amsterdam, Basle, Paris, the principal towns of Germany, Scandinavia, Austria, and Czecho-Slovakia, which thus became part of its European network.

The inauguration of the first air-mail service took place in April 1930. On February 23, 1935 the first aircraft flew the Belgian Congo link-up in 5½ days. Now at least one daily plane leaves Brussels for Belgium's overseas territories, making the trip in an average of 16 hours.

Progress in the Congo continued at the same rate. The air network had to be considerably extended, the operational area spread wider, connections speeded up, flying time reduced, and transport capacity increased in order to keep up with the ever increasing demand for service.

At the outbreak of war in 1940 SABENA's total network, covering Europe, Africa and the Congo inland system, measured 11,250 miles. In Europe alone this network covered over 3,731 miles in summer and 1,292 miles in winter. The fleet of machines numbered 40; five of the 30 pilots had flown together well over 625,000 miles and four more than 468,750 miles. In 1938, the last pre-war year of normal operations, SABENA set up these records: 34,110 passengers and 837,584 T/km. freight and mail carried; 2,082,030 miles flown.

SABENA's activities in Europe were provisionally stopped when the nazi troops marched into Belgium. The air fleet escaped to Great Britain, the workshops were dismantled and all immovable equipment destroyed. Nothing but empty hangers remained when the invaders reached Brussels.

SABENA's planes were at once placed at the disposal of the Allied Armies and were used for supply work in England and France. Two Savoia-Marchettis and one DC-3 were shot down while returning from a military mission. The remainder of the fleet was sent to North Africa under the command of the French Air Minister, and shortly afterwards taken by the enemy.

There still remained the air power in the Belgian Congo: 7 Fokker F — VII's and 6 JU 52's. Towards the end of the summer of 1940 SABENA devised an air-link Albertville-Cairo via Nairobi; a few weeks later followed the opening of the route Takoradi, Acora, Lagos, Bengui, Stanleyville, Khartoum, Cairo. Twice a week throughout the war this air line was used for carrying Allied military chiefs, troops, arms, munitions, foodstuffs and medical supplies. SABENA crews flew with-

In the service of Pan American, this DC-4 "Clipper" carried forty four.

out respite or rest, covering in some cases 34,375 miles in one month.

The fleet was increased by the acquisition of fast Lockheed XIV's and Lodestars. The network was again extended to the Cape and Johannesburg, and in 1945 the company's planes in Africa were making regular flights over 20,000 miles. Two months after V-day the Belgian Congo was once more united by air with the Motherland. SABENA had again proved its power of recuperation, and once more confirmed its vitality. A few weeks later, repeating the performance of its early days, SABENA attacked the skies of Europe, and by the end of 1945 had renewed its connections with London, Paris Stockholm and other Western capitals.

Less than a year later the company's pre-war position was well surpassed. The first four-engined DC-4's which had been added to the fleet helped largely in the relief of the colonial population. In due course SABENA inaugurated new lines, including the transatlantic service Brussels-New York in 1947, and services to Israel and Naples (Italy).

The company was first in Europe (1947) to operate the famous four-engined DC-6 with pressurized cabins, and was thus able to fly the fastest service to the Belgian Congo (16 hours) and to the Union of South Africa (Johannesburg, 24 hours). SABENA was also first (1949) to use the two-engined "Convair Liner" on its European network.

The first postal service by helicopter on the Continent was started in 1940 by SABENA in cooperation with the Belgian Post Office. The service was carried in three Bell 47 Di helicopters. During three years of operation these machines carried 166 tons of mail (some 33-35 million letters) on daily flights with a total length of 438 km. and including landings in eight towns.

Soon the pioneer role of the Belgian air lines in using rotating-wing aircraft led to the acquisition of at first three, and later four, helicopters S-55, and to the inauguration of the first regular international passenger services by helicopter.

At the end of one operational year these machines had transported, 13,000 passengers on three international lines: Brussels-Antwerp-Rotterdam; Brussels-Liege - Maastricht - Cologne - Bonn; Brussels - Lille, and 5,000 passengers on chartered and special flights. By May 1, 1955 SABENA's helicopter experience showed a record of 15,000 flying hours and well over 20,000 passengers.

In view of this success the Belgian Air Lines decided to put another two machines into service (Spring 1955) and to plan the extension of the network to Eindhoven, the Ruhr and the Southwest coast of the Netherlands.

In 1953 SABENA bought six four-engined Douglas DC-6B's in order to meet the increased demand following introduction of tourist class on its entire network. The following year two more four-engined DC-6C's were added to the fleet. This type of aircraft is particularly suitable for mixed cargo and passengers services; it takes 38 tourist class passengers and 4 tons of freight.

At present SABENA's total network covers 150,000 km., including 35,000 km. in Africa. A link-up of the Atlantic ocean with the Indian Ocean (Dar-es-Salaam) has now been added to the African network. The fleet contains 79 fast modern machines.

Commercial development has closely followed this increase in power and traffic. The Belgian air lines fly to 36 countries on 4 continents, serving 99 towns; the commercial set-up includes 34 offices in the United States, South Africa, Great Britain, Germany, Italy and Israel.

With an annual turnover of some B. frs. 2,000 million SABENA has become one of the largest national concerns. The Belgian air lines rank among the first ten airways of the world.

SABENA's president M. Gilbert PERIER was elected president for 1948-49 of I.A.T.A. (International Air Transport Association), one of the international organizations of which it is a member. M. PERIER has since been on the board of I.A.T.A.

Over 37 years of experience enables SABENA to do a job which fulfills in the largest possible measure the needs of Belgium's economy in a framework of world-wide air connections.

The Caravelles VI and the Boeing Intercontinentals constitute the new generation of Sabena's air fleet.

The first generation, from 1924 to 1938, was that of the 3-engine machines. Next came the generation of the twin-engine and 4-engine aircraft assigned respectively to middle-distance and long-haul traffic. The jet machines now in service open a new era in which commercial speeds are nearing the speed of sound.

A Law Three Centuries Old

The new jet-engines make it possible to reach any point on the earth in less than a day. This is modern enough, but it has its origin in a law which is an old friend in the physics laboratory. It is a law first formulated by Isaac Newton (1642-1727) — "Every action has an equal and opposite reaction." Its effect is familiar to every child who demonstrates it indeed, when he lets the air out of his toy balloon. As the air escapes in one direction, the balloon jumps off in the other.

A jet-engine is called in French, a "reaction engine." It works on this same principle of a jet of gas and is so constructed that the jet is maintained. The jet itself, is the "action." The equal and opposite reaction is the forward thrust which carries the aircraft through the air.

Newton's law is so old established that it is hard to know when it was first applied in practice. Moreover, it is a delicate task to attribute this advance to any particular person for it is a matter in which national prides and prestiges are involved. It was not until nearly the end of the second world war that the first jet engines of consistent characteristics, and capable of series production, were put on the drawing board. They were to power fighter aircraft; but before long they were to be brought into more peaceful uses.

The development of the piston engine had virtually reached its limit. It had become impossible to increase the power any further without a disproportionate increase in the dimensions, the complexity and the rotation speed, of engines in this class. Moreover, the rotation speed was limited by the use of the air screw, the extremities of which would lose their effectiveness if they were to pass the sound barrier.

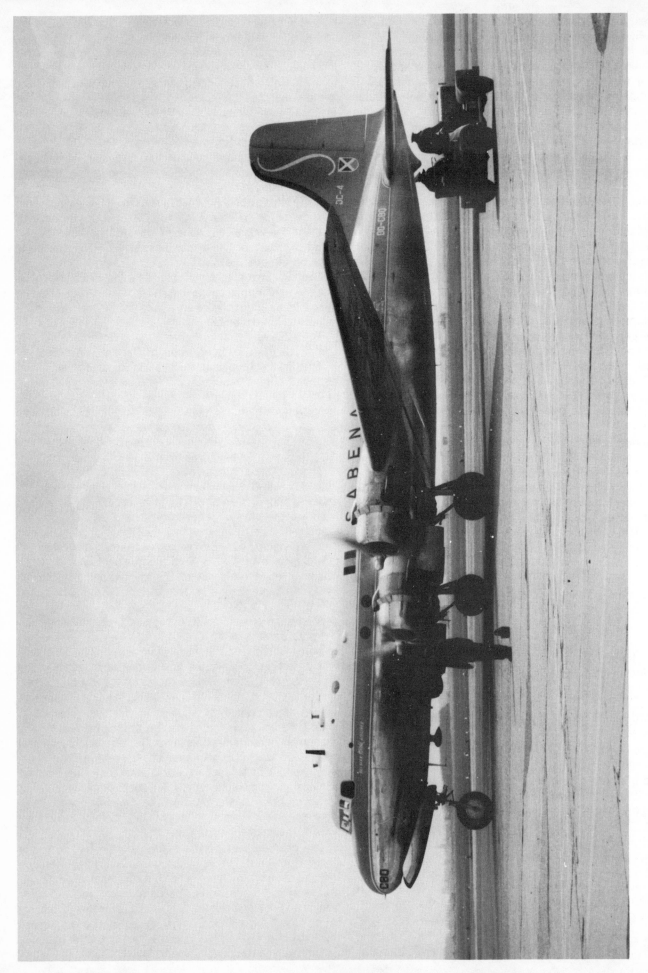

Douglas DC-4, like its predecessor the DC-3, has been seen under many flags. Here Sabena Belgian airlines DC-4 warms up at Brussels National Airport.

The jet engine has made it possible to conquer new velocities. Added to this is the previous work on pressurization which has made it possible for aircraft technicians to design machines to fly at 10,000 meters altitude or over.

A new task for them was to adapt the form of the aircraft to its new speeds. It is this which led to the arrow shape of the swept wing — the only way of getting through the air at such speeds without vibration.

Middle and Long-Distance

From the beginning SABENA traffic had been in two forms. On the one hand, there were long-haul services such as Belgium-Congo and, since the end of the war, Belgium-North America and Belgium-South Africa. On the other hand were the shorter flights such as those of the company's European service and the flights to the Middle East.

This sub-division exists for all airline companies. It has led to both the companies and the aircraft constructors making a definite distinction, particularly since World War II between the aircraft suitable for the different lengths of flight.

The middle-distance aircraft operated by SABENA since 1946, have all been twin-engine machines. In chronological order, they were the Douglas DC-3, the Convair liner and the Convair Metropolitan. At the same time, the inter-continental lines were operated successively by the 4-engine Douglas DC-4, DC-6 and DC-7C.

A new requirement was for machines suitable for shorter distances. SABENA was the first airline company to deal with this by acquiring a fleet of helicopters and by using them to operate an international network in Western Europe.

SABENA has now chosen two new types of aircraft with characteristics best adapted to the company's two types of activity. In choosing them, it has been guided by the necessities of commercial competition, by the desire to offer consistenty the best possible service, and to fulfill its national and international mission.

The names of these two types are now well known. On the one hand there are the 4-jet American aircraft Boeing Intercontinental; and on the other the French twin-jet machines Caravelle VI.

The first, since 1960, has been linking Brussels with Leopoldville, with Johannesburg, with New York, with Montreal and with Mexico.

The second, has been brought into service on the middle-distance lines in the European network and between Brussels and the Middle East.

Less than two years ago, all the SABENA services were carried in piston-engine aircraft. Today the new jet aircraft, the Boeings and the Caravelles are responsible for more than half the Belgian Company's production. There are in fact 12 jet aircraft — 4 Boeing Intercontinental 4-jet machines and 8 twin-jet Caravelle VI — and in terms of ton-km. facilities produced, they represent 62% of SABENA's production. There are still 68 piston engine aircraft which are responsible for the other 38% of the traffic facilities produced.

This is indication enough of the importance to the Belgian airline company of its jet fleet which, in the spring of 1962, will be increased by an additional two Boeing 707 aircraft.

The Company's fleet is given an extremely detailed overhaul at regular intervals, so as to maintain it in perfect flying trim, and to make sure that the passengers are safe and comfortable. This is the main preoccupation of the management, and it requires all the qualities of faultless organization resulting from 38 years experience in commercial aviation.

The maintenance and overhaul programs are drawn up by specialist departments, guided by the requirements laid down by the manufacturer and in some cases by the experience of other airline companies. These programs are first submitted for approval to the Belgian Aeronautical Administration.

Northwest Orient DC-4 cruises at 246 mph over the fields of Minnesota.

Boeing *Stratoliner* set "deep chested" trend in transports for a while, was first pressurized cabin craft, Pan American put this model in service between Miami and San Juan in 1940.

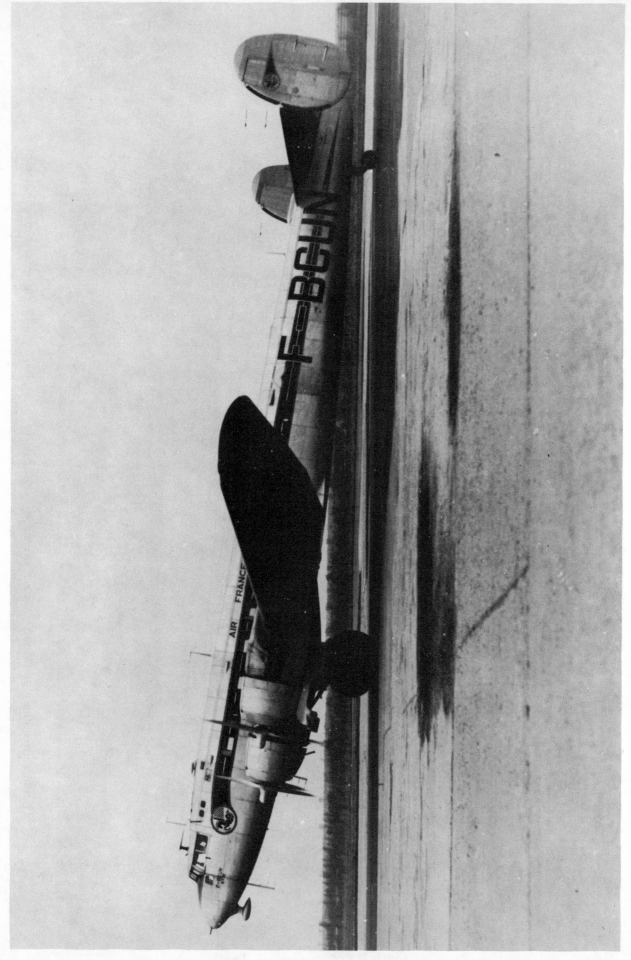

Air France Bloch 161 bore superficial resemblance to DC-4, but did not approach it in speed (205 mph cruising) or capacity (thirty two).

More look-alikes for the Douglas *DC-4* were the Focke-Wolf Condor 200 (above) and the Junkers *JU-90* (next page). Condor carried forty at 185 mph.

Junkers JU-90, like Focke-Wolf Condor (preceding page) operated by Lufthansa, was somewhat faster at 201 mph cruising, had same capacity.

Big Air France Breuget *Provence* was cargo/transport/troopship design, could handle 107 passengers, maintain 248 mph cruising speed.

TWA's Martin 404 twin engined craft were roughly equivalent to DC-4 in speed and capacity.

SWISSAIR

CIVIL AVIATION had its beginnings in Switzerland in January 1919, when Major Arnold Isler, then commander of the Swiss Air Force, set up an air service between Zurich-Duebendorf and Berne-Oberlindach. Swiss-built military planes of the type Haefeli DH-3 were used, flown by Air Force pilots.

At first they carried only military mail between Air Force base at Zurich and Army Headquarters at Berne. Experience that had been gained with air links between Berlin and Weimer in Germany encouraged Major Isler to take a further step. At the beginning of February he extended the service to Lausanne and at the end of April to Geneva. At the same time he put it at the disposal of the public. At first only mail was admitted, but from June the service also carried passengers. The single-engine DH-3s, which had a maximum still-air speed of about 120 km/h, had room for one passenger in the open observer's seat behind the pilot. The flight from Geneva to Zurich with stops at Lausanne and Berne took two hours and twenty minutes and cost 300 francs. After a trial period of six months, during which a total of 23,530 pieces of mail and 246 passengers were carried, this first Swiss air service was suspended on 1st, November 1919. Technically and operationally speaking, the result had been satisfactory; only the hope to cover the costs from revenue had not been fulfilled.

But in the same year three private air transport companies were formed. In the middle of April the Aero-Gesellschaft Comte, Mittelholzer & Co. was founded in Zurich, followed on 25th, June by the Avion Tourisme S.A. in Geneva. At the beginning of July the former chief flying instructor of the Swiss Air Force, Lieutenant Oskar Bider, formed a "Committee to promote a Swiss company for air Tourism" which led on 20th, September to the foundation in Zurich of Frick & Co. This third company became on 15th, December the Ad Astra Swiss Air Transport Company with a capital of 300,000 francs. However, the existence side by side of three companies all with the same aim meant an uneconomic splitting of efforts. Therefore, the board of Ad Astra AG decided in February 1920 to buy up Comte, Mittelholzer & Co. and in April of the same year Avion Tourisme S.A.

The new organization took the name "Swiss Air Transport Company Ad Astra Aero, Avion Tourisme S.A." or in short Ad Astra Aero. The head office was in Zurich, and a branch office was located in Geneva. The share capital amounted to 600,000 francs. The fleet numbered sixteen aircraft: seven Macchi-Nieuport and five Savoia flying-boats, three German L.V.G. land-planes and a Condor for aerial acrobatics. In 1920, the first business year, the Company's seven pilots made 4,699 flights carrying 7,384 passengers. The operation of the flying-boats brought, however, heavy financial losses. On 1st, June 1922 Ad Astra opened the first line from Switzerland abroad, from Geneva to Nuremberg via Zurich, using a Junkers F-13, the first real

transport had thus entered the international field.

In September 1925 a second air transport company was founded in Basle with a capital of 100,000 francs, called Basle Air Transport AG Balair. With a fleet of six Fokker aircraft it ran regular services between Basle and Stuttgart, Frankfurt-Karlsruhe-Basle-Geneva-Lyons and Basle-La Chaux-de-Fonds.

Three years later Ad Astra decided on an outstanding pioneering deed: with a Dornier-Merkur it opened, in pool with the German Lufthansa, the first European "express-service" on the 680 km route Zurich-Berlin, which was then the longest non-stop service in Europe. The flight took about five hours.

On 26th, March 1931 Balair and Ad Astra decided to merge into an undertaking for the whole of Switzerland and founded with a capital of 800,000 francs the Swiss Air Transport AG Swissair. The new company owned eight three-engine Fokker F-VIIb, two single-engine Dornier-Merkur, one single-engine Fokker F-VIIa, a single-engine Messerschmitt M-18d and a single-engine Comte AC-4, totalling 86 passenger seats. The small number of air crews comprised ten pilots, seven radio-operators and eight flight-engineers. Operations were carried out only in the summer season, from March to October, and then only under favorable weather conditions. The route network totalled 4,203 km.

Under the able management of Balz Zimmermann and Walter Mittelholzer Swiss civil aviation now made great strides. In the middle of April 1932, Swissair, as first European carrier, started to operate planes built in America. They were the speed-planes of the type Lockheed-Orion which caused quite a sensation. Their cruising speed reached 260 km/h, or 100 km/h more than any other plane then in use in Europe. Powered by a Wright-Cyclone engine of 575 HP, this low-wing monoplane had a range of 950 km. With payload of 815 Kg. it accommodated four passengers apart from the pilot. On 2nd, May Swissair inaugurated with its two Lockheed-Orions an express service from Zurich to Vienna via Munich. The distance of 610 km required an average only 140 minutes! The commercial success was outstanding: the load factor averaged 82 per cent. The purchase of the Orions contributed materially in making Swissair known throughout Europe and in inspiring confidence in the young Company.

In 1934 Swissair put into service as further innovation a twin-engine American aircraft of the type Curtiss-Condor, which had room for 15 to 16 passengers. To look after what was at the time a high number of passengers, aboard an aircraft, Swissair employed stewardesses, again the first European carrier to do so.

After an interruption of almost six years, caused by World War II, Swissair resumed services on 30th, July 1945 and enlarged the fleet by the acquisition of several DC-3s. In the following year it ordered four Douglas DC-4s, its first four-engine planes.

During the war enormous technical progress had been made in the construction and equipment of aircraft. At the same time, rail and road transport had

Douglas DC-6 became United "Mainliner" on cross-country runs.

suffered severely from war damage. In shipping, too, there was a great shortage, notably in transocean vessels. In these conditions air transport made very rapid headway and expanded into all parts of the world to an extent no one had foreseen. Flights across the North Atlantic and over other long distances were no longer very difficult. The keen demand for transport prevailing in the immediate post-war years opened new fields of action also to Swissair. Air transport was about to develop rapidly into a world-wide industry; every effort had to be made to release Switzerland completely from the shackles of its geographical position and to secure its participation in world air traffic. It was with these new perspectives in view that the General Meeting of the Company decided on 26th, August 1946 to raise the share capital to 20 million francs.

In February 1947 Swissair became officially the national airline of Switzerland, with some State participation. Public institutions took over 30 per cent of the share capital, while the other 70 per cent remained in private hands. On 2nd, May of the same year, an aircraft of Swissair, a DC-4, flew for the first time from Geneva to New York. Regular North Atlantic services however, were not started until the end of April 1949 after further proving flights. This route was later to become the economic backbone of the Company.

On 27th, May 1954, Swissair opened as part of the long-haul program a new route leading from Zurich and Geneva to Rio de Janeiro and Sao Paulo in Brazil, with calls at Lisbon, Dakar and Recife. This route has also proved very successful.

In 1957 Swissair's network, which in the preceding year totalled about 58,000 km, will again be expanded. The most important event in this program is the setting-up of a route to the Far East via Geneva, Athens, Beirut/Cairo, Karachi, Bombay, Bangkok and Manila and a second route from Zurich via Geneva, Athens, Beirut, Karachi, Calcutta, Bangkok and Hong Kong, both routes terminating in Tokyo. The South America route is being extended to Buenos Aires. Additional North Atlantic services are operated via Lisbon. Stockholm and Cologne join the European network. In the Near and Middle East, Swissair has for some time been flying to Athens, Istanbul, Tel Aviv, Beirut, Damascus and Caito; now its planes will also land in Bagdad and Dhahran. All these additions bring the network length to 74,000 km.

Air traffic is now in full development and will no doubt maintain its up-trend in the coming years. Swissair is determined, in the interest of the Swiss economy and tourist trade to do everything possible to secure for our land-locked country full participation in the modern world traffic routes of the air. It is no less determined to consolidate and to expand further the position it has won through quality and service in over 25 years of hard competition. It has set itself a task requiring the greatest effort, but which for that very reason is all the more worth achieving. At the same time a new field of action is being opened to our young people offering them employment with excellent prospects.

Overwater hops were routine for the *DC6-B*. Northwest employed them on Honolulu run.

Consolidated Vultee Convair 240 was workhorse equivalent to DC3 for many lines.

Convair 240 was chosen by KLM as one of basic transports with which to rebuild after WWII. A forty-place ship, it cruised at 272 mph.

Convair 340 picked by Lufthansa for use when air operations were resumed, neared 300 mph with fifty two aboard.

Braniff Airways was flying Convair 340's in 1952 when this photo was made.

DC-6 in service of American Airlines, shown over New York City, carried sixty eight passengers.

147

The DC-6B, here in Sabena trim, carried four fewer passengers than the DC-6, but cruised at 315 mph, compared with 285 for the earlier model.

TRANS-CANADA AIR LINES

THE RAPID development of aviation in Canada over a comparatively short period is dramatically summarized in the story of Trans-Canada Air Lines. In just 24 years (it was formed in 1937) TCA has expanded its routes from 122 miles to more than 30,000, and as Canada's national air service has made impressive air transport history.

TCA, a publicly owned company, was incorporated by Act of Canadian Parliament in April, 1937. The airline was formed to co-ordinate air transport across the broad expanse of Canada and to help provide facilities for Canadian international air service.

Prior to 1937, there had been much pioneering activity in the air in Canada, but nothing of a trans-continental design had developed. Operations were of the bush variety serving isolated northern communities and mining camps out of reach by surface transportation. Schedule flights were limited to some on the Pacific Coast into the Northwest Territories and Yukon, along the north shores of the St. Lawrence and throughout the Maritimes.

To remedy the lack of co-ordinated air service, TCA came into being. It was intended directly for the rapid carriage of passengers, mail and goods, and indirectly for the further integration of a nation of tremendous distances. By employing the skills of a people with an innate feeling for the air, by absorbing the bush pilots and the aviation pioneers into the wider pattern and by continuing an air transport tradition that had long since become legendary, the work was quickly done.

TCA began with almost nothing in 1937. Airport, navigation and communications facilities adequate to support scheduled services by large aircraft were largely non-existent.

On July 7, 1937, the first survey flight of the proposed transcontinental route took off from Vancouver for eastern Canada. This marked the beginning of operations.

In September of the same year, TCA began its first commercial service over the 122 mile route from Vancouver to Seattle.

Then work was begun on experimental flying and training in western Canada with 10-passenger Lockheed Electras as equipment, and less than 100 employees as staff.

Progress then came quickly. A pattern of radio range stations was spotted across Canada by the Department of Transport. Meteorological services were established by the same Government organization. Late in 1938, after extensive training over the Rockies and on night operations, airmail and express were moving transcontinentally between Montreal and Vancouver.

On April 1, 1939, schedule passenger service was inaugurated between Montreal and Vancouver and between Lethbridge and Edmonton bringing transcontinental air transportation to Canadians for the first time. Early in 1940 services were opened into the Maritimes. Larger Lockheed 14 aircraft, were added to the fleet.

Early in the war, events moved swiftly as the company commenced building up a pattern of Canadian inter-city services. And again larger aircraft, this time 14-passenger Lockheeds, took to the air wearing the maple leaf insignia.

In 1943, TCA first spanned the Atlantic. At the request of the Canadian Government, trans-Atlantic service was established to provide for the rapid transport of priority passengers, armed services' mail and cargo. Converted Lancaster equipment was used.

The immediate post-war period saw an unprecedented rate of TCA growth. Many ex-service personnel were brought into the airline and were trained as pilots, mechanics, radio operators and other specialists. A new twin-engine fleet of 27 DC-3's, which carry 21 passengers, replaced the Lockheeds. New and important extensions of routes were made to both Canadian and United States communities.

Early in 1947 the modernization of the fleet began with the acceptance of the first of twenty 4-engine North Stars. These aircraft were built in Canada, based on the Douglas DC-6 design and powered with Rolls-Royce engines designed for high altitude flight. They had accommodation for 40 passengers in pressurized cabins and space for the transporting of 7,500 pounds of mail and cargo. Later eight seats were added with no loss of passenger comfort.

The arrival of the North Stars signalled a new chapter in TCA history. They were first put into service on the North Atlantic in the summer of 1947 as TCA's overseas operations assumed full commercial identity. The new equipment brought greater load capacity and increased speed and comfort, making it possible for TCA to greatly augment its air transportation services both domestically and internationally until the present extensive route pattern was attained.

In 1954, a number of North Stars were adapted to contain 54 seats and a Tourist service on a twice daily round-trip basis trans-continentally was inaugurated. In 1955 the seating configuration was increased to 62.

Trans-continental air transport has provided Canadians and their goods with new mobility and has helped overcome the last physical barriers to national unity and understanding. Its speed has helped knit a nation which is almost clumsily big into something more compact and manageable. TCA's North Stars reduced coast to coast travel time, over a distance in excess of 3,000 miles, from the 6 days of a decade ago to less than 20 hours. Winnipeg, situated at the geographical center of the continent was only 5 hours from the Pacific coast and 6 from Montreal, the stepping off point for Europe. All the North Stars were sold in 1961.

In 1954, Super Constellation aircraft made their appearance on the North Atlantic routes of the Company. For the first time in history of TCA, both first class and tourist service was offered air travellers in the aircraft across the North Atlantic.

TCA, in company with other great world carriers, has also contributed to economic and social intercourse on an international scale by bringing the world's communities into closer proximity.

On April 1, 1955, regularly scheduled flights of

Convair's Metropolitan (440) appealed to Swissair for its European operation.

Vickers Viscount turbo-propeller aircraft were introduced domestically. Their advent marked the first time that propeller-turbine power was offered to the travelling public of North America.

The first scheduled Viscount route operated between Montreal and Winnipeg with enroute stops at Toronto and the Lakehead (Fort Williams-Port Arthur). On April 4 trans-border Viscount service between Toronto and New York was inaugurated. Trans-continental Viscount service between Montreal and Vancouver was inaugurated November 1.

The traveller with limited time at his disposal is no longer confined to the narrow radius of his home area. For a Canadian, the entire nation, or even the whole of the globe, lies just beyond his nearest airport.

Air transportation has done more than just diminish the importance of distance for the potential passenger. It has also served as a stimulus to industry and business. Air Freight is enlarging markets, opening new ones, bringing about entire new concepts in merchandising and helping to keep the wheels of industry in motion. It also provides for the carriage of airmail to facilitate the rapid movement of ideas and information.

On November 1, 1955 service was extended in the Province of Quebec, bringing a new balance to an already comprehensive national route pattern. This occured when TCA exchanged its Toronto-Mexico City service for Canadian Pacific Airlines' Quebec and Northern Ontario routes. This permitted the inclusion of six more centers in the national air network. Also, service was provided between Quebec City and the Maritime provinces for the first time.

In 1955 the company introduced tourist air service to Florida, Bermuda and the Caribbean. Also, family fare plan rates were extended to the trans-Atlantic flights for winter travel.

The first of 11 ordered Douglas DC-8 jetliners for service on transcontinental and intercontinental routes, was delivered to the airline on February 7, 1960. Capable of carrying 127 passengers at 550 miles an hour, this aircraft makes the journey from Vancouver to Toronto in less than five hours; from Montreal to London, England, in just over six hours. TCA now flies only DC-8's between Canada and the United Kingdom and between Canada and continental Europe.

Vickers Vanguard turbo-prop aircraft went into service on transcontinental routes in February, 1960, to the Atlantic Provinces April 30, and to New York and Chicago June 15.

The Vanguard is a 96-passenger, 425-mile-an-hour airliner powered by four Rolls-Royce Tyne turbine engines, ideally suited for medium and short-stage air routes. Its distinctive "double-bubble" fuselage — a cross-section of which gives the appearance of a flattened figure "8" — contains cargo holds below the passenger deck capable of carrying up to 10,000 pounds of freight, express and mail when passenger loads are light.

The airline's initial order early in 1957 for 20 Vanguards costing $67,100,000 was, at that time, the largest single export dollar order placed in postwar Britain. Since then, three additional Vanguards have been ordered. To date, 18 have been delivered to the airline.

TCA plans call for standardization to three basic types of aircraft — Viscounts, Vickers Vanguards and Douglas DC-8s — and expects to possess the world's first completely turbine-powered intercontinental air fleet by early 1962.

To maintain and overhaul the DC-8 and Vanguard, TCA has built at Montreal the world's first maintenance and overhaul base designed exclusively for turbine aircraft, at a cost of more than $20,000,000. Viscounts are overhauled at Winnipeg. A $3,500,000 line maintenance base for turbine aircraft has been built at Vancouver, and a similar one $1,500,000 base is under construction at Halifax.

TCA ranks as one of the world's largest international commercial air carriers, serving 39 Canadian communities; six cities in the United States; Trinidad, Jamaica, Barbados, Antigua and Nassau in the Caribbean; Bermuda; and London, Glasgow, Shannon, Dusseldorf, Vienna, Paris, Brussels, and Zurich, in the United Kingdom and continental Europe over 30,000 miles of air routes.

United Airlines Boeing *Stratocruiser* got above weather to cruise at 300 mph.

Boeing *Stratocruiser* was high-altitude choice of Pan American Airways.

Lockheed Turboprop *Electra* was transition plane from propeller driven to pure jet transports, exceeded 400 mph.

Vickers *Vanguard* is analgous to *Electra*. Sleek ship carries up to 139 at 435 mph.

Candair *North Star* was Canadian-built version of Douglas DC-6, first introduced in 1947. This is Canadian Pacific craft.

TRANS WORLD AIRLINES

WHEN TWA, early in 1950 changed its corporate name from Transcontinental and Western Air, Inc., to Trans World Airlines, Inc., the change in official designation reflected the great expansion of the company.

The country's oldest transcontinental airline, TWA has been offering the public a reliable schedule air service since 1929. Early in 1946, it added 21,000 miles of overseas routes to its 11,000 miles of domestic routes. Now the red "TWA" sign, familiar in cities half way round the world, is the designation of a globe-girdling service, operating as Trans World Airlines.

It was in 1925 that Western Air Express, the earliest of TWA's "parents", was organized to bid on an air mail route from Los Angeles to Salt Lake City. By April of the next year, WAE was carrying both passengers and mail over this route on regular schedules, the first time such combined air service ever had been offered the public.

Later in 1926, two young pilots, Jack Frye and Paul E. Richter, organized Aero Corporation of California, a combined flying school, service and maintenance base, and airplane sales agency. The following year Aero corporation went into the airline business by forming Standard Air Lines, a subsidiary originally operating a single passenger airplane between Los Angeles and Tucson (Arizona).

A third predecessor of TWA came into being also in 1927. It was Maddux Air Lines which operated the world's first fleet of all-metal planes (Ford tri-motors) between Tijuana (Mexico), San Diego, Los Angeles and (later) on north to San Francisco and southeast to Phoenix.

While these three pioneering airlines were expanding in the West, the general public first was shocked into a fuller realization than ever before of the possibilities of flight when, in 1927, an unknown named "Slim" Lindbergh left New York and landed some 33 hours later in Paris, to become an international hero.

The next year saw the organization of the last of TWA's parental foursome, Transcontinental Air Transport, by the "Keyes group" headed by C. M. Keyes, a prominent financier of that day. The new firm, formed specifically to inaugurate the nation's first high-speed coast-to-coast air-rail service, was financed to the tune of $7,500,000 with the Pennsylvania Railroad holding the largest interest.

After hiring Lindbergh to survey its transcontinental route, T-A-T inaugurated, July 7, 1929, its combined plane-train service. Passengers on the journey rode an overnight Pennsylvania Railroad train bewteen New York and Columbus, flew by day from Columbus to Waynoka, Oklahoma, boarded a train there for an overnight ride to Clovis, New Mexico, and the next morning flew on from Clovis to Los Angeles, completing the transcontinental trip in the then phenomenal time of 48 hours. The coast-to-coast fare was $351.94. ($157.85 in 1950; $110 by Skycoach).

TWA's parents began to get together in 1929. T-A-T obtained control of Maddux Air Lines, thereby extending its service to San Francisco. Soon Western Air Express, operating daily flights all over the West, Southwest and as far east as Kansas City, absorbed Standard Air Lines.

Finally, on October 1, 1930, Western Air Express, headed by H. M. (Pop) Hanshue, and T-A-T Maddux, led by Jack Maddux, completed a merger, and Transcontinental and Western Air, Inc. (TWA), was born. Each parent firm received 47.5 per cent of the stock, with 5 per cent going to Pittsburgh Aviation Industries Corporation, owner of the Pittsburgh-Butler airport, a key point in the new system's plans. Hanshue was the first president, and Keyes, leading T-A-T promoter, became chairman of the board. Jack Frye of Standard and Western Air was the new firm's vice-president of operations.

Only 25 days after its formation, TWA gave up its rail connections and began operating an all-air transcontinental service. Even though passengers flew only in the daytime, staying overnight in Kansas City, the new service cut the coast-to-coast time to 36 hours.

In April 1931, after Richard W. Robbins had succeeded Hanshue as President, TWA took one of the many aggressive steps in its history by acquiring fast Northrop single-engine mail airplanes and flying them on a 24-hour transcontinental schedule, the fastest such service of that day.

TWA's passenger fleet then included tri-motor Fords, often nicknamed the "tin goose"; both single and tri-motor Fokkers, and two big, lumbering, 32-passenger Fokker 32's, the first four-engine airplanes ever flown by a U. S. airline.

By 1932, TWA's operations department had solved the problems of night flying, and the line began transporting passengers as well as mail from coast to coast in 24 hours.

But TWA pilots and executives, not satisfied with this performance, wanted better airplanes and improved passenger service. The old Fords and Fokkers were too slow, too noisy, too lacking in passenger comfort.

Since no suitable new types of aircraft were then in prospect, TWA embarked on a policy that was to give it undisputed leadership both in aircraft operated and in the development and use of technical flying aids: — If you can't buy one already made, design one yourself.

Following that policy, TWA engineers went to work with the Douglas Aircraft Company to design a new, modern passenger airplane. The result was a single prototype airplane (DC-1) delivered to TWA in 1933. D. W. (Tommy) Tomlinson, TWA pilot and later TWA Vice-President of Engineering, conducted an exhaustive five-month test-flight program with the DC-1 which resulted in quantity production of an improved and refined model, the 14-passenger DC-2, to be followed by the famed 21-passenger DC-3, renowned in the late war (as the AAF C-47 and the Navy R4D) and long a standby for most United States Airlines.

TWA was the first operator to adopt the DC-2, buying an original fleet of 31. Putting them in operation in 1934, the airline again led the field in reducing trans-

Douglas DC series of propeller aircraft continued with *DC-7*, carrying ninety five passengers at a cruising speed of 355 mph.

continental flying times — this time to less than 16 hours.

Perhaps the greatest crisis for TWA — and for other airlines, too — was the wholesale cancellation of air mail contracts by the government early in 1934.

In its original corporate form, TWA not only lost its air mail contracts but like other lines, was also ineligible to bid for new contracts when the routes were reassigned.

The only answer for TWA was a corporate reorganization. This it accomplished in two steps. First (April 1934) it organized a new firm, called TWA, Inc., which promptly entered bids for new mail contracts. Then, in December of that year (1934) TWA, Inc., and Transcontinental and Western Air, Inc., consolidated under the name of the latter.

The interim firm carried the mail over a portion of TWA's routes from May 13 until December 27. Nearly six years passed, however, before TWA regained all of its original air mail contracts, and this extended pinch on revenues proved a heavy financial burden as time went on.

Since the air mail cancellation edict barred the heads of all airlines from future participation in the air mail business, TWA had to find a new president to replace Richard W. Robbins. The man selected was Jack Frye, then executive vice-president, and later to become president of TWA, Inc. Henry B. duPont was elected chairman of both firms.

Another shift in the TWA fortunes came when new laws, enacted just after the air mail crisis, divorced the transportation and manufacturing interests of the aviation industry, thus forcing General Motors to withdraw from TWA (GM had held a major interest in Western Air Express). The controlling interest then passed over to John D. Hertz, Sr., the Yellow Cab magnate, and Lehman Brothers, where it remained until 1938.

The ensuing years found TWA, now free of corporate troubles, concentrating on technical research and development, looking toward improved aircraft and better flying aids. It was during this time that Tommy Tomlinson conducted his exhaustive research program into the mysteries of high-altitude, "over-the-weather" flight. From this exploration came data which led to production of the Boeing four-engine Stratoliner, first transport airplane with cabin pressurization, a development permitting smooth over-weather flying at altitudes of 14,000 feet and more with cabin pressure equivalent to only half that figure.

Again TWA had pioneered in the air transport field and was the first and only domestic airline to put these modern, four-engine land planes into service. With the Stratoliner, flown in 1940, TWA cut the transcontinental flying time to 14 hours.

Despite the financial struggles which plagued all industry during the 1930's, TWA never faltered in its drive for technical progress, and its record is full of vital safety and operational aids developed or first used by the airline.

Among these, TWA was first to establish its own meteorological department (1929), first to develop and use de-icer equipment (1932), first to adopt the automatic pilot (1934), first to use wing flaps (1934), first to develop and use the automatic direction finder and the anti-static radio antenna.

During April, 1938, control of TWA switched again, this time to the airline's officials and exactly a year later it was revealed that Howard Hughes, multi-millionaire manufacturer, movie-maker and pilot, was TWA's principal stockholder, through his control of the Hughes Tool Company, which owns the majority of TWA's stock. Stockholders other than those representing the Hughes Tool Company on August 10, 1948 voted more than 16 to 1 in favor of a TWA proposal to allow the Hughes Tool Company to convert a $10,000,000 loan into TWA common stock at $10 per share. A proposal to increase the authorized shares of TWA common stock from three to four million was also carried overwhelmingly.

Even before the Stratoliners were flying, TWA was seeking an airplane that would carry huge loads across continents and oceans at a speed of 300 miles an hour. TWA, Lockheed and Howard Hughes, in 1939, collaborated on the design of such an airplane. The result was the beautiful and renowned Constellation, holder of more speed and safety records than any four-engine transport plane now in commercial service.

Though delayed by the war, the "Connie" was first flown in January 1943, going immediately to the Army which used it and succeeding units produced until the war's end.

Meanwhile, TWA pointed its efforts toward winning the war. It had been the first airline to make its facilities available to the government — in the summer of 1940, a year-and-a-half before Pearl Harbor — and when hostilities actually began, TWA turned over its fleet of Stratoliners, and later its Constellations, to the Army. In February 1942, TWA became the first domestic airline to operate land transports overseas for the Air Transport Command.

From that month until the end of the war, TWA's Intercontinental Division operated 9,800 overseas contract flights for the ATC, carrying vital war materials and personnel abroad, and returning with airplane loads of wounded. In addition, the airline trained hundreds of Army pilots in the operation of four-engine aircraft plus hundreds more men in technical specialties.

Before victory came, TWA saw its hopes of acquiring an international route become a reality. Knowing that in the Constellation it had an excellent over-ocean airplane, TWA had planned and applied to the Civil Aeronautics Board in 1944 for a 'round-the-world route.

On July 5, 1945, the CAB certificated TWA to fly from the United States across the North Atlantic to the British Isles, Europe, North Africa, the Middle East, India and Ceylon.

Creating an International Division with headquarters in New York, TWA chalked up the first over-ocean Constellation flight from Washington to Paris December 3, 1945, and only two months afterward, on February 5, 1946, regular New York-to-Paris service was inaugurated. Ten days later TWA's Connies began speeding across the continent on schedules in less than 10 hours.

International service was extended to Cairo, April 1, 1946, and to Lisbon and Madrid on May 1. Chicago-

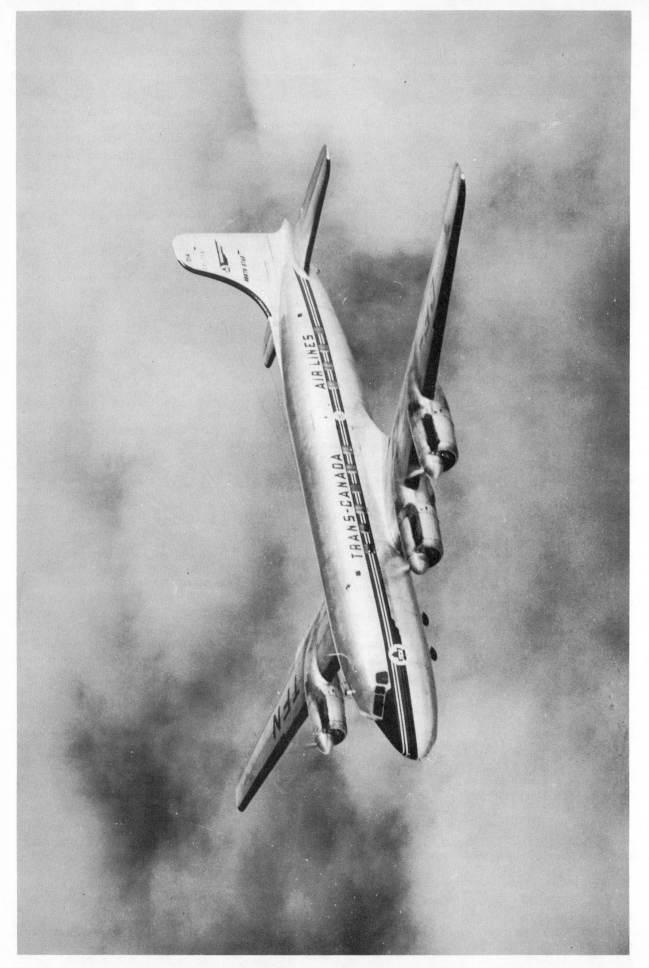

North Star has been refined upward to seat sixty two instead of original forty. Pressurized cabin allowed first high altitude flights by Canadian airlines.

to-Cairo flights were initiated May 3. On January 5, 1947, TWA inaugurated service to Bombay.

Twelve days later the airline pioneered again when the world's first international all-cargo flight, TWA's "Shanghai Merchant", took off from New York bound for Cairo. This weekly round-trip all-cargo service since has been extended to Bombay.

Also on the foreign scene, TWA lent technical assistance to the Ethiopian Air Lines and the Saudi-Arabian Airlines; it assumed a small or minority financial interest in TACA (The Latin-American carrier), the Philippine Air Lines, LAI (Linee Aeree Italiane), and TAE (Greek Airlines).

On August 1, 1946, the CAB granted TWA the right to provide service as far east as Shanghai, connecting there with Northwest Airlines' route across the North Pacific to Chicago. With that action, most, if not all, of TWA's globe girdling dreams had come true. Despite all the notable accomplishments of 1946, the year also brought a full measure of troubles to TWA. In July the Constellation fleet, then totaling 16 airplanes, was grounded until a number of expensive modifications were completed. Not until early October were the Connies flying again.

Hardly had the company begun to recover from this crisis, when the entire TWA system was paralyzed by a three-week pilot strike. Large financial losses during the year, arising principally from these two major difficulties and the costly development of overseas routes, precipitated a reorganization of the company early in 1947. Jack Frye, President; T. B. Wilson, Chairman of the Board, and Paul E. Richter, Executive Vice-President, among other officials, resigned. Thirteen new directors were added to the 11-member board in January, serving until the company's annual meeting April 24. As of April 1, 1950, the TWA board numbered 14 members.

TWA's reorganization in 1947 culminated in the election of Warren Lee Pierson, TWA Director and President of American Cable and Radio Corporation, as Chairman of the Board; and LaMotte T. Cohu, then Chairman of the Board and general manager of Northrop Aircraft, Inc., as President of the airline.

The present TWA route structure — embracing more than 32,000 miles from California eastward to India — serves the four continents of North America, Europe, Africa, and Asia.

Spreading a network of swift, dependable transportation from the West Coast cities of San Francisco and Los Angeles to New York, Boston, and Washington, TWA by 1950 was certificated to serve 60 cities within the United States.

From Los Angeles to New York, air travelers can cross the United States on one-stop Constellation flights in 10 hours and 10 minutes. Or, preferring a more leisurely flight, they can visit cities rich with history, industrially thriving, such as Las Vegas, Phoenix, Winslow, Albuquerque, Santa Fe, Amarillo, Wichita, Topeka, Kansas City, Quincy, Hannibal, Peoria, and Chicago.

On TWA routes, travelers can visit St. Louis, Terre Haute, Indianapolis, South Bend, Fort Wayne, Louisville, Cincinnati, Dayton, Columbus, Pittsburgh, Harris-burg, Lancaster, Reading, Allentown-Bethlehem, Silmington, and Philadelphia.

Other TWA routes serve Williamsport, Wilkes-Barre and Scranton, Albany, Worcester and Boston.

On the Los Angeles-San Francisco segment, the traveler has aerial access to Burbank, Fresno, Oakland, and San Diego.

The present domestic route pattern represents a four-fold expansion since 1936 when TWA served 15 cities.

Many of the new routes and cities added since 1936 offer "feeder traffic" to the main TWA transcontinental routes and enable the airline to operate with higher load factors and increased passenger and cargo revenue.

By interchanging equipment with Delta Airlines at Cincinnati, TWA is also authorized to provide one-carrier service to the South and Southeast from Detroit, Toledo, Dayton and Columbus, Ohio.

A domestic airline until World War II, TWA became global-conscious soon after Pearl Harbor when it contracted with the Army Air Transport Command for certain of its airplanes and crews to fly vital material and personnel in trans-Atlantic service.

This wartime experiment in over-ocean flying opened entirely new horizons for the airline which had begun to push its way eastward from California in 1925. No longer was it content to be hemmed in by the boundaries of North America. In competition with previously established international carriers, it applied for and received routes that made TWA truly the Trans World Airline.

On July 5, 1945, the Civil Aeronautics Board, with approval of the President of the United States, awarded TWA a certificate to provide international air transport on two routes: (a) from New York and other large cities in Northeastern United States to Ireland, France, Switzerland, Italy, Greece, Egypt, Palestine, Iraq, Saudi-Arabia, India and Ceylon; and (b) from the same United States terminal cities to Portugal, Spain, North Africa, Egypt, and thence to the Near East and the Far East.

Later, the CAB authorized TWA to extend its service from India to Shanghai, but at present the company is flying only as far as Bombay.

The present overseas routes serve 16 cities in 14 countries on four continents.

In the wake of postwar expansion, TWA in 1947 was confronted by a need for a strengthened financial position and for the means to acquire new aircraft.

In the management change in April of that year, TWA found the needed financial acumen in its new Chairman of the Board, Warren Lee Pierson, international financier and businessman.

LaMotte T. Cohu, President of TWA until his resignation on June 1, 1948, aided in directing the company. From June 1948 until January 25, 1949, Mr. Pierson was chairman of the Executive Committee which was responsible for the mangement of the company.

Under new management, TWA concentrated on cost reduction and on consolidation of the airline. The domestic system had been operating on a regional basis, while the international service had a separate organization from the domestic service. These were brought together into a unified operation.

Second version DC-7B incorporated minor modifications, cruised at 360 mph.

During 1947 TWA completed a financing program for the purchase of new aircraft. Five DC-4s were added to the TWA fleet, four new Constellations were placed in domestic service; another 12 long-range Constellations, to be delivered the following year, were purchased for overseas service.

Passenger miles flown in 1947 increased to 1,043,761,000 from the 852,998,000 of the year before.

By the end of 1948, TWA was able to report that traffic had increased another 15 percent — while costs had been pared. Costs per ton mile, a yardstick for the measurement of economy in air transport operations, was reduced to 39.91 cents from 42.15 per available ton mile in 1947. With its 12 new Constellations flying overseas, TWA was able to transfer and add eight Constellations to its domestic routes and to inaugurate Constellation Air service into Washington, Dayton, Philadelphia, Pittsburgh, Albuquerque and other cities.

On January 25, 1949, Ralph S. Damon assumed the presidency of TWA.

One of the few men in the United States to be president of four major corporations, he brought to the company knowledge of both aircraft manufacturing and airline operations. Before his TWA presidency, he was president of Curtiss-Wright Airplane Co., Republic Aviation Corp., and American Airlines.

Since the large losses of 1946 (adjusted net loss, $8,987,000), TWA had been steadily strengthening its financial position. Adjusted net losses decreased from $5,377,000 for 1947 to $1,278,000 for 1948. At the close of 1949, Mr. Pierson and Mr. Damon were able to report that TWA had turned the corner with a profit of $3,709,000.

Nineteen forty-nine marked the year in which air transport came of age. On July 9 of that year, TWA, the country's oldest transcontinental airline, celebrated the 20th anniversary of its coast-to-coast service.

In the year 1949 TWA acquired, or made arrangements for, new aircraft that was to give it the world's largest fleet of standardized postwar four-engine aircraft. The airline determined upon the use of the Constellation — a 300-mile-an-hour airplane with a proven record of fast, dependable performance.

TWA ordered 26 new Constellations for long-haul traffic. For short-haul flights on its domestic routes, it ordered, early in 1950, 30 of the new Martin 404s and arranged to lease 12 Martin 202s for use before the delivery of the 404s. The twin-engined Martin 404 is designed so that it can be converted to jet engine driven propellers.

In September 1949, TWA inaugurated a restyling program of the interiors of the 35 Constellations then in service in its fleet. This was the largest program of its type ever undertaken by a commercial airline. Installing the most modern passenger comforts in its airplanes, TWA at the same time increased seat capacity in order to offer uniform service over its 32,000 miles of routes.

For 1950, TWA's total fleet (including aircraft on order) included 61 Constellations — the world's largest fleet of postwar four-engine commercial aircraft. Its other aircraft were: 30 Martin 404s (on order) 12 Martin 202s (on order for leasing); 14 Douglas DC-4s; 58 Douglas DC-3s, and five (5) four-engine Boeing Stratoliners.

On its transcontinental service, TWA in 1949 inaugurated a "Skycoach" or low-cost, transcontinental service. During the less busy months of the year on its international routes, it encouraged overseas travel by reducing trans-Atlantic fares. To its overseas terminals, it added Zurich, Switzerland, and resumed service to Israel in 1949, after the latter service had been temporarily suspended by hostilities. Early in 1950 it added Milan, Italy to the overseas cities it serves.

The year 1961 brought significant changes to Trans World Airlines, including a change in top management and expansion of the Super Jet fleet.

The year will be remembered as the one in which TWA became the only U. S. carrier operating jet aircraft exclusively across the North Atlantic. TWA also took the lead in backing President Kennedy's campaign to encourage tourists from other lands to visit the U. S. A.

TWA activity accelerated in March, when an eight months' vacancy in the president's office was filled by Charles C. Tillinghast, Jr., former vice president of international operations for the Bendix Corporation. Mr. Tillinghast was elected by TWA's reconstituted board of directors. The new board includes prominent men from the U. S. business and industrial scene. Ernest R. Breech, former board chairman of the Ford Motor Company, became TWA's board chairman.

Changes on the board of directors followed the passing of control from the Hughes Tool Company to a three-man voting trusteeship as part of a financing program with a group of banks and insurance companies. The voting trustees named to vote the 78 per cent of TWA stock previously controlled by Hughes Tool Company were Mr. Breech, Raymond M. Holliday, vice president of Hughes Tool, and Irving S. Olds, former chairman of U. S. Steel.

In May TWA announced purchase of 26 more Boeings powered by advanced Pratt & Whitney turbofan engines for delivery between mid 1962 and early 1963. Also during 1961, TWA leased four new 720B turbofan jets from Boeing for domestic use until after delivery begins on the new turbofan fleet.

The overall business decline in 1961 affected TWA along with most other carriers. Combined passenger volumes for TWA's domestic and international divisions dropped 5½ per cent from 1960. One service within TWA that showed marked increases was air cargo, with ton miles up 26 per cent over 1960.

Commenting on the need to improve the airline's financial condition, Mr. Tillinghast proposed a 5 per cent increase in coach fares to stem the diversion from first class, and recommended an increase from 40 to 66 pounds in the free baggage allowance for first class domestic passengers; in addition, he proposed a one-dollar increase for each passenger ticket and a 5 per cent increase on first class fares for trips on piston planes of less than 1,200 miles. This, he said, would help bring the airlines closer to the 10.5

Long haul DC-7C used by KLM to Near East carried sixty two in luxury.

per cent return on investments that the CAB itself determined to be appropriate.

Changes occurred at the operations level as TWA continued to establish industry-leading standards of performance. Floyd D. Hall, formerly vice president and general transportation manager, became senior vice president and system general manager. He replaced E. O. Cocke, who advanced to senior vice president of industry affairs. Mr. Hall's former position was filled by J. E. Frankum, who had been general transportation manager for the Atlantic Region.

Continuing its technical leadership, TWA this year commenced use of the revolutionary Doppler navigational system on its trans-Atlantic aircraft. Doppler, which provides precise navigation without the use of ground radio aids, is the most significant development in trans-Atlantic navigation equipment since the sextant was invented.

In 1962 TWA will become the first commercial air carrier to use the complete automatic Doppler system tied into computers and operated by pilots.

In jet on-time performance, TWA substantially outstripped its principal domestic competitors. Departures were as much as 77 per cent and arrivals up to 75 per cent on-time, even during periods of heaviest travel. This was 10 to 20 per cent better than the competition. TWA's international on-time reliability showed marked improvements.

On-time performance was greatly aided by TWA's technical services staff, which maintains the jets. TWA maintenance reached such proficiency in 1961, that the Federal Aviation Agency granted the airline unprecedented extensions in the length of time it can operate its turbojet engines between overhauls. TWA's crew training program, already recognized as an industry model, was further improved in 1961 with the order for another $1,000,000 flight simulator.

This unit will give TWA six such simulators, more than any other airline. Even the Military Air Transport crews that fly President Kennedy's jet came to TWA in 1961 for proficiency training on the simulators.

Having achieved a position second to none in quality of flight equipment and service, TWA moved forward to match these with comparable ground facilities by opening its modern, spacious terminal in Los Angeles as a forerunner to openings of spectacular new terminals at Chicago O'Hare and New York International Airports early in 1962.

TWA is forecasting not only general business improvement for 1962, but an improvement in its own position relative to the airline industry. Optimism comes partly from the jet fleet expansion, giving TWA 12 jets for international service versus nine in 1961. Also, the new TWA terminals in three major markets — Los Angeles, Chicago and New York — will place TWA in a better competitive position both domestically and internationally.

Lockheed Constellation also flies under many flags. Here QANTAS Connie is high over rugged terrain.

EL AL Israel Airline Constellation was one of the first long range craft acquired by young company.

Super G Constellation in service of KLM handles up to ninety nine passengers.

Air France Vickers *Viscount* has 300 mph. cruising speed.

Continental Vickers *Viscount II* is distinguished by "porthole" windows.

Boeing 707 has become standard for many airlines.

Lufthansa uses 707's on New York-Frankfurt non-stop run.

United's first DC-8 jet rolls out from Douglas factory at Long Beach. Announced price of these craft was $5,000,000 each. Passenger capacity: 116 to 151.

Swissair DC-8 soars above clouds at 554 mph.

UNITED AIR LINES

UNITED AIR LINES is observing its 35th anniversary this year as the nation's senior airline tracing its origin to Varney Air Lines. This pioneer carrier was awarded an air mail contract by the U. S. Post Office in 1925, and on April 6, 1926, Varney began operations between Pasco, Wash., and Elko, Nev. This is regarded as the beginning of scheduled air transportation in the United States.

Climaxing 35 years of service improvement and company growth, United on June 1, 1961, substantially expanded its system with the merger of Capital Airlines into United.

The merger provided United with new routes in the East and South, and expanded the system to 116 cities in 32 states, British Columbia and the District of Columbia, along an airline network of 18,000 route miles.

The new United Air Lines is flying more than 250 aircraft along the Main Line Airway, including two turbojet types, the Douglas DC-8 and the Boeing 720, the turboprop Viscount formerly operated by Capital, and the DC-7, DC-6/DC-6B and Convair.

The merger also has accounted for a sizeable increase in the United personnel "family," from 23,000 to more than 30,000. The company's executive headquarters adjacent to Midway Airport will move at year's end to a new site near Chicago's jet age airport, Chicago-O'Hare International. United's operating base is in Denver and its maintenance base for centralized fleet overhaul in San Francisco. Viscount overhauls are performed at the company's Washington, D. C. maintenance facilities.

The early history of United reflects the birth of the air transport industry. A dozen or more fledgling airlines took to the skies in 1926-27. The largest was Boeing Air Transport, which inaugurated service between San Francisco and Chicago in July, 1927. Pacific Air Transport, operating between Seattle and Los Angeles, was acquired by Boeing Air Transport in 1928. United Aircraft & Transport Corporation was formed the following year as the holding company for these two airlines and other aviation interests.

National Air Transport, which flew the Dallas-Chicago-New York route, became a division of the holding company in 1930, along with Varney Air Lines. An integrated coast-to-coast system now became possible. United Air Lines was organized in 1931 as the management company for Boeing Air Transport, Pacific Air Transport, National Air Transport and Varney Air Lines.

United Air Lines became a separate, independent company in 1934. W. A. Patterson, who previously had headed the four operating divisions, was elected president and he has served in that capacity to the present day. Under his guidance, the company has achieved its present stature, serving communities from the Atlantic to the Pacific, from Boston to Miami and New Orleans, the length of the Pacific Coast into Canada and from California to Hawaii.

For jet age operations, United has committed upwards of half a billion dollars for 39 Douglas DC-8s, 29 Boeing 720s, 20 Caravelles, 40 Boeing 727s and spare parts. The DC-8 Jet Mainliner, which entered service in 1959, is designed for long-range schedules. In comparison, the Boeing 720, introduced in 1960, flies medium distances. The French twin-jet Caravelle, a mid-1961 entrant, is designed for short and medium haul service along with the Boeing 727, which will enter service late in 1963.

United has expanded its San Francisco Maintenance Base for the jet fleet, building a turbine-engine overhaul plant and other facilities. The base is presently expanding its technical force to reach 4,300 employees by the close of this year. In 1960 the base overhauled 160 airframes and 1,147 engines. Near the base on a 40-acre site is the company's new Jet Service Center for line maintenance of jet aircraft.

The Denver Operating Base often is described as the nerve center of United's system. Special techniques developed there enable management to plan each day's operations in terms of weather conditions, traffic fluctuations and other factors. Operating statistics covering the entire system are posted in a briefing room for daily review and analysis.

The fastest and most accurate reservations service ever developed is provided by the "Instamatic" system introduced by United this year. The largest integrated data processing system in commercial use, it permits handling of 80 per cent of all reservations in less than one second. Three thousand United sales agents in 100 locations are linked by high-speed communications with the company's Reservations Control Center in Denver.

United has the world's largest concentration of electronic flight simulators at its Flight Training Center at Denver and was the first to install a DC-8 jet simulator for airline use. With delivery of a Caravelle simulator this year, the equipment will consist of two DC-8 flight trainers, one Boeing 720, one Caravelle, three DC-6Bs and one Convair 340. The first DC-8 training aid has closed-circuit television which projects a realistic airport in front of the cockpit during simulated landings and take-offs.

Scheduled to open later this year is a new "airline university" near Chicago's O'Hare International Airport. The largest and most complete facility of its kind in the industry, the training center will be used for instruction of supervisory personnel and stewardesses.

United established the world's first flight kitchen at Oakland, Calif., in 1936 and now operates the largest airline commissary department. Sixteen flight kitchens prepare 8¼ million meals and snacks annually for serving aloft.

In advancing to its present stature, United has been responsible for many "firsts." The first airline stewardesses, for example, were hired by Boeing Air Transport in 1930. The company made the first experimental installation of automatic pilots in 1933 and in 1938 was first to install two-way coast-to-coast telemeter service. More recently, United was first to equip its entire fleet with C-band weather-mapping radar.

In systemwide 1960 operations United carried 8,111,000 passengers and 143,000 tons of mail, express and freight.

Sud Aviation Caravelle, twin jet, is fast, smaller transport.

United's Caravelles seat ninety one passengers, skim through sky at 575 mph.

Mid range jetliner is typified by Boeing 720 with its one hundred passenger capacity and 600 mph speed.

Long range 707's are employed by Air France, here coming in to land.

Sabena, Belgian airline, is still another user of 90-place 707's.

How fast is fast, these days?

FAST THESE DAYS, for most people, is about 600 mph in a modern jet.

Last year, some 25 million people really went places at that speed. Some 4 million whisked across the Atlantic in 6½ hours. (If you're interested, Columbus did it in 1,734 hours.) Another 4 million flew across the American continent in 6 hours.

On Braniff, we flew our share of these gadabouts over several jet routes: Chicago to Dallas, Minneapolis/St. Paul to Mexico City, and the like. One of them, New York to Buenos Aires, is 5,297 miles—farther than New York to Moscow, but just over 13 hours of flying time.

Man, the slowpoke

The interesting thing about all this is the speed with which it came about. Assuming that *homo sapiens* has been developing for well over 8,000 years (and we like to count on several thousand more for him to keep up the good work), his success with speed has occurred in only 1/100th of the time he's had.

As late as 1880, the cheetah was still speed king among mammals. That noble animal was clocked at 70 mph, recently. We assume he could do the same in 1880, when men were able to sprint at 20, float in a balloon at 25 (if the wind was right) and ride a horse at 40. The railroads were coming up on the outside, however. In 1893, Engine 999 of the New York Central ate up a stretch of track near Batavia, N. Y., at 112.5 mph. Hail to the new king.

Enter 2 brothers, from the wings

Then came Orville and Wilbur Wright in 1903. They weren't really speed demons — at Kitty Hawk, they flew 852 feet at only 9 mph — but they had the *wright* idea.

To us, their plane looks like an

On the subject of speed: of planes, of sound, of progress...What's coming in the future—and how fast.

orange crate with a room fan in front. But planes got better and faster, quickly. When Braniff opened for business in 1928, five aeronauts (including crew) flew from Tulsa to Oklahoma City at a daring 90 mph. Not up to the railroads, but coming along.

In 1936, the Age of Speed got a boost from the appearance of the classic DC-3. Thousands of people began to get from here to there at 175 mph. Splendid and faster DC-4's, 6's and 7's followed.

Jet out of town

In the 40's, the British developed the prop-jet engine — a combination of the propeller principle and the jet principle. Newer, U.S.-built prop-jets, such as those Braniff flies, cruise at over 400 mph.

Remember: a plane with a cruising speed of 400 mph is scheduled at much less—so it will have reserve power to overcome headwinds and still arrive on time.

Then, in the 50's, came the pure jet, based on the startlingly simple notion that a stream of compressed air and gas, expanding, would give enough forward thrust to fly at great speeds. Interestingly, the faster a jet goes, the easier it is to produce more thrust. And the higher it goes, the less thrust it needs. Potential jet speeds are nearly unlimited. (One of our Braniff jets just happens to hold a speed record for commercial airliners—805 mph.)

The sound of music—how fast?

When airlines say they fly at "about" or "near" the speed of sound, they aren't trying to be vague. The problem is that sound goes at different speeds at different altitudes. 760 mph at sea level; 663 mph at 40,000 feet. (Much like a horse on different footings.) One would expect sound to travel faster, higher, where there is less resistance. Not at all. Sound needs something to go through. In air, the more the better.

Here comes the future

These days, Air Force jets breeze along at 1,500 mph with the greatest of ease. (At last look, the experimental X-15 was doing 4,093—fast enough to cross the continent in 36 minutes.) There's a sign-post for the future. In 20 years, we suspect it will be a commonplace to "beat the time zones"— leave, say, New York on a Braniff jet and arrive in Dallas before you took off, by the clock. (English grammar isn't ready for it, but we are.)

If 1,500 mph seems extreme, remember that we are already going 66,600 miles an hour — the earth's speed in orbit. Venus steps along at 78,400 miles an hour. Light at 186,000 miles *per second*. We have a long way to go!

Recently, we heard of a woman who phoned 1,000 miles on a Friday to suggest that her grandchildren fly out for the weekend. They did— and we think there will be more of that. What's more, we think more people all over the world should get around to see each other faster, more often. If they get around more often, they'll get along better.

We therefore salute our grandchildren, who will fly faster.

BRANIFF *International* AIRWAYS

Huge Douglas DC-8C carries up to 154 people, maintains 589 mph cruising speed.

Boeing 707 "Golden Jet" flies high over Rocky Mountains on Continental's Denver-Los Angeles run.

Delta Airline DC8-50 is powered by Pratt & Whitney JT3D turbo fan engines with 17,000 lb. thrust.

Alitalia DC-8 has been called "Flying Art Gallery" because of original contemporary Italian paintings adorning the bulkheads. Luxurious interior was designed by distinguished Professor of Architecture at Padua University.

BAC One Eleven twin jet with unique tail configuration is scheduled for September 1963 delivery to Braniff.

QANTAS, whose AVRO was the first pictured in this historical resume, now gives passengers ten times the speed and a plane capacity fifty times as great as that which it offered a short forty years ago. Such has been the progress of airline transportation in the era from Jenny to Jet!